INTRODUCTION TO THE
PEER REVIEW ORGANIZATION

INTRODUCTION TO THE
PEER REVIEW ORGANIZATION

▼

Lisa Raymond, RN, BA, LNC

Writers Club Press

San Jose New York Lincoln Shanghai

Introduction To The Peer Review Organization

Writers Club Press
an imprint of iUniverse, Inc.

For information address:
iUniverse, Inc.
5220 S. 16th St., Suite 200
Lincoln, NE 68512
www.iuniverse.com

ISBN: 0-595-20680-8

Printed in the United States of America

To my husband Tim Decker and
Our three sons
Andy, Tyler and Nick

CONTENTS

▼

FOREWORD

Any time medical information is used in a public setting, care must be taken to protect the confidentiality of the patient. Therefore, I have changed minor details, locations or other distinguishing characteristics of the patients in this book. Details needed to illustrate a point or medical diagnoses remain intact.

Medical errors are an emotional subject for any practitioner whether or not they have ever been accused of substandard medical practices. Physicians and other medical personnel that were subject to peer review and sanctioned for the poor quality of the medical care given have also been protected. I have changed minor details to protect their identities and myself from legal action.

This book is not about medical errors, but about the process of reviewing medical care that uncovers the errors and the actions that are taken after errors are discovered. It is also about reimbursement procedures for government paid medical services. Both issues are important to medical professionals and the hospitals where they practice.

ACKNOWLEDGEMENTS

▼

Many nurses and other medical professionals provided valuable contributions for the completion of this book, whether they knew it or not. I would be remiss not to acknowledge the contributions of Pam Gardner Hector, who helped me to learn the ropes while I was employed at the Illinois Medicaid PRO. Her insight and grasp of the issues involved in utilization review are impressive.

Meredith Fay and Eve Springer provided expertise in their specialties of pattern profiling and panel reviews, as well as, moral support. Also, Meredith supplied the coffee and Eve provided the chocolate when things got rough.

Marcia Humes and Christie Delaney not only provided friendship and support, they asked the right questions when I was needed it most.

Penny Revell did what she does best, which set me on the right path.

Other people that provided information and support are Kay Thomason, a Certified Coding Specialist, who made sense of the numbers for me and taught me to think like a coder, instead of a nurse, when DRGs are the issue.

Renee Potter, MPH, who guided me through the focused quality studies and accepted me on the diabetes team.

Dr. Herman Langner who taught me how to keep my sense of humor and perspective.

And Marylyn Gagliardo, former CEO of the Illinois Medicaid PRO, who showed us all how to do a tough job with integrity and grace.

--------------▼--------------

CHAPTER ONE

THE PEER REVIEW ORGANIZATION

The medical profession is very much aware of the need for defensive documentation in the medical record in the event of legal action. A malpractice or professional negligence lawsuit may be brought against the professional years after the care was given and the medical record may be the only evidence available for an effective defense. Memories fade and the medical record is tangible evidence of the medical care received by the patient.

However, many nurses and other medical professionals are unaware of another audience looking at the documentation in the medical record for quality of the medical care and medical necessity issues. This audience is much more likely to review the record than an attorney or a judge. This audience reviews hundreds of thousands of medical records every year and failure to meet their standards can result in severe sanctions.

Nurses have been reprimanded, fired or their cases sent to state licensing boards as a result of external reviews. Physicians have had their licenses placed on probation or even revoked after a review organization determined the physician's practices did not meet medical standards of care.

Hospitals have been sanctioned and/or denied millions of dollars in reimbursement for medical services provided to patients. Intensive auditing may also result from the external review process. At a time when many hospitals are struggling to survive, the loss of reimbursement from the government programs can mean the difference between keeping the doors open or not.

Medicare and Medicaid pay millions of dollars every year for health care services for recipients of the government health programs. After qualifying as a Medicaid or Medicare provider, facilities and physicians are eligible to bill claims for services to the government programs. However, there are some conditions that must be met.

First, both Medicare and Medicaid have predetermined rates of reimbursement for services. The predetermined reimbursement rate can, and often is, less than the actual cost of providing the care. The medical care provider must agree to accept the payment schedule set by the government programs, regardless of the cost of delivering the care.

For Medicaid recipients, it is illegal to seek further payment from the patient for any shortfall. However, Medicare patients are responsible for a co-payment whenever they receive medical care. Medicare supplement insurance covers the out-of-pocket expenses and co-payments not covered by Medicare. If the recipient does not have supplement insurance, the expenses are the responsibility of the patient.

For acute medical care, reimbursement is based on Diagnostic Related Groups (DRG). Each medical condition is assigned a DRG code that corresponds to a set payment. The payment is for the entire hospital stay. For a patient that is in the hospital five days after a myocardial infarction (MI), the payment is the same for a patient in the hospital four days after the MI.

Diagnosis codes for inpatient care using the ICD-9 system may be three to five digits and the most specific diagnosis code must be used. For example, 440.2 is the code for atherosclerosis of the native arteries of an extremity. Code 440.21indicates atherosclerosis of the extremity with claudication. Code 440.22 is for intermittent claudication and 440.24 is the code for atherosclerosis of an extremity with gangrene. If the atherosclerosis is in a grafted vessel, the code is 440.30 for an unspecified graft.

For patient admitted for atherosclerosis of the right leg with intermittent claudication or pain at rest, the correct code would be 440.22. There may be additional codes for other conditions, such as diabetes or coronary artery disease and procedure codes for the hospital stay. The atherosclerosis is the reason for the admission, so it is the principal diagnosis used. Code 440.2 is technically correct, but not specific enough to be used.

For psychiatric care, chemical dependency detoxification and acute medical rehabilitation, the payment may be based on *per diem* payments. For each day the patient is in the hospital, the facility is compensated a set amount each day. The amount is predetermined based on the type of care given. Psychiatric care may pay more than detoxification, but less than medical rehabilitation. Reimbursement is set by the government program and can be different for each region that is covered by the program. Hospitals that provide emergency psychiatric care, while the patient is being prepared for transfer to another facility for psychiatric care, can bill using the DRG codes.

The second condition for reimbursement by the government programs is peer review. Each time a bill is submitted to the program, either Medicare or Medicaid, the care is subject to peer review for quality of care, appropriate utilization of services and accurate DRG coding of the claim. This is where the Peer Review Organizations come into the picture. The organizations do the reviews for the government.

In order to protect recipients from unnecessary care, care that is too restrictive an environment (this is mainly for psychiatric care) or poor quality of care, the government programs contract with Peer Review Organizations (PRO) who provide oversight of the care given to recipients in all areas of health care. Some review organization review for both Medicare and Medicaid and some review for only one of the programs.

For example, in Illinois, the PRO for Medicaid reviews a percentage of acute care medical claims based on the principal diagnosis DRG code. In a given fiscal year, the PRO looked at all the cases in which a diagnosis was on a list of conditions to receive close scrutiny.

The conditions on the list included such diagnoses as gastroenteritis and circumcision. The diagnosis did not have to be the primary reason for the admission. In addition, 100% of acute psychiatric services, 100% of acute detoxification and 100% of acute medical rehabilitation claims are reviewed prior to authorization of payment. All one-day stays, for any reason, are also reviewed.

In 2000, the Illinois Medicaid PRO reviewed over 90,000 hospital admissions for both quality and utilization standards. They also reviewed medical records from managed care organizations that had signed up with the Medicaid program to provide services to the Medical Assistance Program.

Although each review organization has different internal policies and deadlines, the overall process and goals for review are similar. The primary goal is to reduce unnecessary medical services provided to recipients and to ensure the care given meets accepted medical standards of care.

The review organization may review a large percentage of the medical care given within their review jurisdiction or may select only a few representative cases. They may have different criteria for selecting cases for review depending on whether Medicaid or Medicare is the payment source.

They may use different terms for each level of review, such as appeal level versus reconsideration level. They also use different titles for personnel involved in the review process, a review analyst in one organization is a nurse reviewer in another. An expedited review at one organization may mean the review is completed within 24 hours. At another organization, an expedited review may mean a different timetable is involved.

Despite differing terminology at the various review organizations, they still have the same goals; reduce unnecessary services that are billed to the programs and to ensure the recipients receive high quality medical care. Uncovering billing errors may also be a goal at an organization.

The review process begins when a bill for services is submitted to one of the government programs. A form is completed in the billing department and sent to the appropriate program for reimbursement. Any mistakes on the form will result in the form being returned and delaying reimbursement.

After Medicare or Medicaid receives an accurate medical claim form, it is entered into the computer system and the claim is either scheduled for payment or selected for a review by the review organization. Medicare uses Fiscal Intermediaries (FI) that are notified of any scheduled medical payments approved by the review organization and the FI is responsible sending the payment.

When a claim is selected for review, the medical care provider is notified that payment is being held until the completion of the peer review process. The selected case is then sent to the review organization. Now, the case is entirely in the hands of the Peer Review Organization for determination of medical necessity and quality of care concerns.

The Peer Review Organization employs physicians, nurses, coding specialists and other medical professionals to review medical records and make decisions on payment, coding accuracy and whether the care was in accordance with accepted medical standards of care.

Nurse-reviewers use government-approved criteria for screening cases or reviewing medical records. In Illinois, Interqual© criteria is used to determine medical necessity for admission. Physicians use their independent medical judgment. Physicians must be actively practicing medicine in their area of specialization and have a non-sanctioned medical license in the state they practice in.

Cases are assigned to physicians based on medical specialty of the physician, care under review, practice setting or subspecialty. A case involving a child treated in a rural hospital for fever of unknown origin would be assigned to a pediatrician that practices in a rural setting, but has no affiliation with the facility where the care was given. If a pediatric infectious disease specialist in a rural practice were available, that physician would be the first choice as a physician-reviewer. Since physicians may have several subspecialties, the closest match to the care under review is used.

The PRO keeps a roster of physician-reviewers that are available to conduct reviews. Each medical specialty is represented, but it is not always possible to have a specialist in every practice area. A pediatric cardiologist in a rural setting is rare, as is a rural radiation oncologist. For these cases, specialty matches are made without regards to practice area when appropriate.

Let's assume the treating physician is a pediatrician, endocrinologist and certified diabetes educator. The pediatrician practices in an urban area. The case under review involves a 4 year old admitted to the hospital after a motor vehicle accident. The child suffered a concussion and tibia-fibula fracture. The pediatrician was on call that night, so assumed care for the child from the emergency room physician. The physician-reviewer selected would be a pediatrician practicing in an urban area without matching the subspecialty of endocrinology since this did not play a part in the child's care.

In the case of an eighty year old admitted to a small rural hospital for pneumonia in which a pediatrician is the only physician on call, the case would be reviewed by an internal medicine or family practice physician. The physician-reviewer would be from a rural practice.

There are physician-reviewers that review very few cases, due to their area of specialization. There are few cases where a dermatologist is the admitting physician or where a pathologist is asked to review a hospital admission. The specialists are available, but seldom needed. In rare cases they are needed to review cases in which care from another treating physician on the case is being questioned.

Other specialists, such as family practice, internal medicine and psychiatry are called on to review frequently. The review organization may be constantly recruiting new physician-reviewers from these specialties in order to keep up with the caseload. Physicians in this specialty may review dozens of charts every month, compared with physicians in less frequently reviewed areas of medicine that review only two or three charts per year.

Although the physician-reviewers use medical judgment, not criteria, they do go through an orientation process. The physician-reviewers are educated regarding what the government programs will and will not pay for. Medicaid does not pay for drug rehabilitation programs, only detoxification. Therefore, if a case is billed as a detoxification case, but the care was actually drug rehab, the claim is denied by the physician-reviewer as a matter of policy.

Nurses employed by the PRO have varied responsibilities and job titles. Nurses conduct screenings of cases to determine whether or not they fail to meet criteria and need a full review by a physician-reviewer. Nurses are assigned to review cases with physician-reviewers, assign cases to the physicians or are managers of departments. Nurses serve on the Board Of Directors of the Peer Review Organization and are Chief Executive Officers.

Some nurses work directly with facilities to educate hospital personnel on the expectations and requirements in the review process. Nurses act as a liaison between the PRO and a facility subject to the review process. Nurses are also responsible for the orientation of physician-reviewers and development of review policies.

CHAPTER TWO

▼

UTILIZATION REVIEWS

The process for determining medical necessity for hospitalization is divided into two areas. Medical necessity for admission for claims billed using DRG codes and medical necessity for admission *plus* medical necessity for the entire length of stay for claims billed on a per diem basis. Most medical services are billed using the DRG system, while psychiatric care is billed per diem.

Claims submitted with a DRG code will be reviewed for both the accuracy of the coding and medical necessity for admission to the hospital. Since DRG claims are a flat fee, the length of time the patient remains in the hospital does not require justification. If the PRO approves the admission to the hospital, every day of the stay is approved.

Once a facility submits a claim for medical services, the government program will decide if the case requires a full review. Many times, the selection is based on the principal diagnosis. If a patient is treated for a condition the government program is looking closely at, it will be reviewed for medical necessity. If Medicare is looking at the care given for gastroenteritis in the hospital setting and a claim is billed with gastroenteritis as the principal diagnosis, the claim will be selected for review.

After the facility is notified that payment is being held until completion of the peer review process, the PRO notifies the facility on what date the medical record must be made available to the nurse-reviewer for screening. The review may be conducted on-site at the facility, or the medical record may need to be copied and sent to the PRO office for an off-site screening.

If the medical record is not available for screening, on-site or off, the review is canceled and the facility must resubmit the claim to the government program and start the process over again. If the medical record is available, the nurse-reviewer screens the case, using the criteria approved by the government program the PRO has contracted with to provide the review services.

If the medical record contains enough information to support acuity for admission, the nurse-reviewer approves the case for payment. The quality of the medical care is also screened at the same time. Even if the care was medically necessary, the case may still be sent to a physician-reviewer if the medical care is not up to standards.

When the nurse-reviewer approves a case under review, the government program is notified and the claim is scheduled for payment. If the medical record does not have enough information to support the decision to admit the patient to the hospital or for a per diem length of stay being billed, the nurse-reviewer notifies the facility of the screening failure. The case must now receive a full review by a physician-reviewer.

The facility is given the opportunity to supply more information for consideration by the physician-reviewer. The additional information may be in writing or the facility can request a telephone conference where the physician in charge of the case can discuss the case with the physician-reviewer. After reviewing the medical record and any additional information provided, the physician reviewer makes a determination whether or not the claim is to be paid.

When the physician-reviewer approves the admission after considering all information available, the approval is communicated to the government program and the case is scheduled for payment. At this level of review, the facility may or may not have supplied additional information.

In many cases, the facility will wait until the physician-reviewer has made a first level determination. If the physician-reviewer approves the case based on the medical record alone, the facility is spared the expense of gathering additional information and submitting it to the Peer Review Organization. This is a more cost-effective way of responding. The appeal is more focused on the concerns of the physician-reviewer because the facility waited for more information from the physician-reviewer as to the reason the case was denied.

When a physician-reviewer determines a patient did not require an acute care admission, the facility is notified in writing of the decision and the medical rationale the physician-reviewer provided as part of that determination. Since the admission was denied, the facility will receive no payment for the admission, unless they appeal and receive a favorable decision at that level.

To conduct an appeal, the facility must supply additional information, either in writing or via telephone conference. If the information is submitted in writing, there is a submission deadline that must be met. If the deadline is missed, there is no appeal and the facility does not receive any compensation for the claim.

If the written appeal is timely, the information and the medical record are sent to an appeal level physician-reviewer. The physician-reviewer must then complete the review within a prescribed length of time to meet deadlines the review organization must meet.

Telephone conferences as a mean of appeal must be requested before the deadline for submission. The telephone conference may or may not be scheduled before the deadline. If the telephone conference is not requested in a timely manner, there is no appeal and the facility is not paid.

As is the case with the first level physician-reviewer, the appeal level physician-reviewer uses medical judgment, not criteria when making a determination. If the reviewer approves the claim at this level, the facility is notified. The government program is also notified so that payment can be scheduled.

If the physician-reviewer denies the claim at the appeal level, the facility receives written notification of the decision and the medical rationale for the denial provided by the physician-reviewer. There are generally no other avenues for appeal. The facility lost the appeal and lost any reimbursement for the services. The facility must now absorb the cost of the patient's care.

For claims billed on a per diem basis, the process is the same, except for one area. If an admission is approved, each day of the admission must also be approved. For a ten-day hospital stay for major depression, after the case meets acuity for admission, the nurse then screens each day to ensure the patient required hospital care on a daily basis. Should the eighth, ninth and tenth day not meet criteria, the case is sent to a physician-reviewer.

The physician-reviewer will look at the three denied days to make a decision on whether or not the patient could have been safely treated in a less acute environment, such as a partial hospital program or outpatient clinic. The physician-reviewer provides medical rationale for the decision and, if denied, it is passed on to the facility.

If only the last day of a hospital stay does not meet criteria, the case will not be sent to the physician-reviewer if Medicaid is the payment source for the case. Medicaid does not pay for the last day of *any* per diem case. It is part of their reimbursement policy.

That is one of the reasons for hospitals trying to get patients discharged early in the mornings. If the patient is discharged at 0800, that day is not paid for, if the patient does not get discharged from the hospital until 1700, the day is still not paid for. It is in the best interest of the hospital to make a non-reimbursed day as short as possible to lessen the expenses that must be absorbed by the facility.

To illustrate the process, assume a Medicaid recipient is admitted to a medium size facility with a mental health unit:

Mr. J is a twenty-seven year old with a history of schizoaffective disorder. Although he is compliant with his medications and outpatient follow-up, he experiences exacerbations of his condition every few months, usually in response to life stressors. He has a difficult relationship with his guardian and frequently requires hospitalization after an argument with the court appointed guardian.

During this admission, Mr. J is having auditory hallucinations telling him to kill himself. He is responding to the internal stimuli and cannot contract for safety. He is placed on suicide precautions with every fifteen-minute checks and his medication is adjusted. He attends all groups and stabilized within eight days. His discharge instructions include follow-up at the local mental health center.

After discharge, the facility, Memorial Hospital, submits a claim to Medicaid for the services provided. Medicaid does not pay for the last day of the stay, so the facility submits a bill for days one through seven.

Sixty to ninety days after submitting the claim, Memorial Hospital receives notification from the Department of Public Aid that the case is on hold pending a review. The state agency has sent the case to the PRO contracted for oversight services. Approximately thirty days later, the facility receives notification from the PRO to send a copy of the medical record to the PRO office by May 1.

The nurse-reviewer screens the medical record when it arrives. The nurse approves the admission based on the inability of Mr. J to contract for safety on the day of admission. The nurse then looks at every day of the stay to determine if Mr. J continued to require inpatient services. Each day of the stay must be justified with information found in the medical record.

During the screening of the entire stay, the nurse-reviewer notes Mr. J denied suicide ideation on day four. There are no progress notes by the physician or the nursing staff containing any information of continued hallucinations or other acute symptoms. All behaviors and problems are chronic in nature for this patient. Chronic care is does not meet criteria for an acute care admission to the hospital.

The nurse-reviewer denies day five through seven and sends written notification to Memorial Hospital of the screening failure. The facility is given the opportunity to supply more information about Mr. J's care. The facility has ten days to submit the additional information before the case is sent to a physician-reviewer. The appeal response is due on May 13.

In this case, Memorial Hospital elects not to respond with additional information at this time. They are confident the medical record contains sufficient information for a favorable determination by the physician-reviewer. After the ten-day deadline, the medical record is sent to a physician-reviewer that is also a psychiatrist that has a practice in a medium size facility. The physician-reviewer has 14 days in which to complete the review.

The reviewing psychiatrist determines Mr. J was stable for discharge on day five. The medical rationale for the decision and the days denied are sent to a nurse in the PRO office. It is up to the nurse to communicate all findings with the hospital or physician involved in the review of a case.

The PRO nurse, in this case called a Medical Review Analyst verifies all the information in the physician-reviewers rationale, reviews the record for any additional concerns and then writes a letter to the facility outlining the denial and rationale for the decision. The denial letter also contains instructions for appealing this decision.

Memorial Hospital now has sixty days from the day the denial letter was sent to request an appeal and supply additional information that will support their defense of the claim. The appeal is due no later than July 28. There are no extensions or exceptions.

At this facility, it is difficult for the physicians to review the medical record and then schedule time to discuss the case with the physician-reviewer, so they send a written appeal. Personnel from Memorial's Utilization Management department drafted the written appeal for this case.

In their appeal, the facility notes the patient's history of frequent exacerbations, even when complaint with treatment. They also noted the severe nature of the command auditory hallucinations on admission, the need for medication adjustments and the risk to the patient if discharged too soon. The treating psychiatrist also signed the letter and added his agreement with the information supplied by Memorial Hospital.

The Peer Review Organization receives the appeal information from Memorial Hospital prior to the deadline. The nurse in charge of coordinating appeals reads the letter and notes that a telephone conference is not requested. The appeal level nurse, also called a Reconsideration Coordinator, adds the letter to the medical record and selects a board certified psychiatrist for the appeal level review. The physician-reviewer has two weeks to complete the review and return the medical record to the Reconsideration Coordinator for processing.

The physician-reviewer considers the letter of appeal and the medical record. The appeal letter does not add any information that is not already in the medical record. The reviewing psychiatrist cannot find any documentation of Mr. J continuing to be a risk to self or others past the fourth hospital day. The length of stay denial is upheld. Hospital days five through seven will not be reimbursed. The facility must now absorb the cost the of patient's care for the denied days.

The nurse in charge of coordinating the appeals receives the medical rationale and decision from the physician-reviewer and verifies the lack of notation regarding Mr. J's risk to himself or others. Mr. J is not suicidal or homicidal and the staff did not note the continued presence of voices or other problems.

The Reconsideration Coordinator then writes a letter to Memorial Hospital informing them of the decision, the medical rationale and the procedure for filing a claim for the days that are approved for payment. Although it is a form letter, it does contain specific information about the patient and the review.

Eight months after the submission of the claim for medical services provided to Mr. J, Memorial Hospital is now free to submit a revised claim for days one through three. Day four is now the last day of the stay and is not paid. There are no more avenues of appeal.

Memorial Hospital must absorb the cost of the denied days and the cost of the appeal. The Utilization Coordinator from Memorial Hospital spent a total of six hours on the case. The Nurse Manager on the mental health unit reviewed the case and provided input and the treating psychiatrist was consulted. A total of 12 hours were spent on gathering information and appealing the denial.

It would be easy to assume from this scenario that Mr. J did not require acute behavioral health services after day five. From the documentation in the medical record, he appears to be stable enough to resume outpatient therapy.

Because this case was selected for review two months after submission of the claim and the first level determination was made one month later, the case was at least three months old when the first denial was received at Memorial Hospital. It may take another month for the UR Coordinator from Memorial Hospital to contact staff involved in Mr. J's care.

The nursing staff on the mental health unit could not remember anything significant about Mr. J's hospital stay that could be used in the appeal. The physician had made notes, but had nothing more to add. There was really not much the facility could offer for a reversal of the denial.

A closer look at the documentation by the nursing staff on the unit reveals scant narratives and flowsheets for suicide precautions, vital signs and attendance sheets for groups. Most of the night shift narratives merely note how often Mr. J was awake during hourly rounds.

The day shift nurses noted attendance at groups and the occasional comment made by Mr. J. There is no mention of discussions held during 1: 1, no mention of how many times Mr. J required redirection for rumination on the internal voices and no mention whether or not he was responding to the voices.

The physician progress notes give detailed comment on medication changes, but no mention is made of Mr. J's response to the changes in medication. The treating psychiatrist does mention Mr. J's willingness to continue treatment in every progress note.

The nursing staff and the physician were very familiar with Mr. J from previous admissions. His previous hospital stays were usually for the same symptoms that prompted this admission. His symptoms and routines were familiar and considered "normal for him."

On day six, when Mr. J paced the halls in agitation over the voices he was hearing, that was standard behavior from him and nobody thought to include it in the medical record. He denied the voices were commanding him to hurt himself and stated they were only making fun of him. The nurses passed on the information during shift report and the physician was aware of the behavior.

When Mr. J could not sleep, he was given relaxation tapes to listen to. The tapes helped him to drown out the voices. Since he did not require medication to sleep, the nurses did not note insomnia in the progress notes, but did pass along in shift report that the tapes were helpful.

If the staff had included these observations in the medical record, the outcome of the review may have been different. If the physician had noted the behaviors and his concern that the patient was still responding to voices, the case could have passed the screening process and never required a physician review at all.

For the physician and the nursing staff, these were obvious signs of continued need for hospitalization. They were well aware of Mr. J's behaviors and history. He was familiar to them. Months later, when asked about Mr. J's stay, the Memorial Hospital nursing staff could not recall anything out of the ordinary, he acted the same as he always did during these periods of exacerbation.

The physician could not recall exactly why he had extended the hospital stay beyond basing the decision on the patient's condition at the time, *which was not documented.* Unfortunately, clinic notes may be less informative than hospital progress notes, but physicians tend to rely more on their clinic notes when asked about a previous admission for a patient.

The physician-reviewer does not know Mr. J and can only make a decision based on information documented in the medical record. The reviewing physician will never see Mr. J and may never talk with the treating physician. Everything is based on the documentation in the medical record.

This sounds like Memorial Hospital has exceptionally poor documentation. In fact, this is common. Documentation at many facilities is internally-directed. All progress notes are written for only one purpose, to keep treatment team members informed of the patient's progress. If something is not written down, it can be passed on during shift report or during a treatment plan meeting. Everyone involved with the patient has an opportunity to talk with other treatment team members during the hospital stay.

The medical professionals reviewing the care for the government paid programs do not have this chance to gather more information. The reviewers will never speak to the patient, never interact with the nursing staff and never see the patient's behaviors. What is a well-known fact internally may never reach a Peer Review Organization and this failure will result in lost revenue for the facility subject to review.

CHAPTER THREE

▼

UTILIZATION PATTERNS AND PROFILING

The review organization profiles medical care providers on a semi-annual or annual basis to look at the rate of denials at a particular facility as compared to the state average for denials. The PRO will enter every payment denial and the reason for the denial into a database. At the end of the profile period, every six or twelve months, the review organization will examine the denials for each facility.

The denial rate and reasons for the denial receive close scrutiny from the review organization. The PRO is looking for patterns. Is this facility frequently admitting patients to inpatient care for observation and not treatment? Does this facility have frequent payment denials for patients waiting for outpatient placement? Does this facility have an average length of stay that is far above the state average?

At the end of a profile period, an employee at the PRO office will generate reports for each facility subject to review by the organization. The reports list overall payment denials; number of denied days, reason for denials and the outcome of appeals. A nurse in the PRO office evaluates the profiling reports.

Any cases in which the over-utilization of medical services was outside the control of the facility are subtracted from the number of denials. All other denials are listed, along with the reason for the denial, and then compared to the state average.

The number of denials is generally expressed in percentages. Facilities that exceed the state average must develop a corrective action plan to decrease the denial rate at that facility.

For example, if the state average for denials is five percent and a facility has a denial rate of seven percent, then a corrective action plan is required. The percentage is based on the admissions to that facility. If there are 15,000 Medicaid admissions in a six-month period and 1050 admission were denied for lack of acuity to meet admission requirements, then the facility has a pattern of unnecessary admissions.

For length of stay, the percentage is based on number of days billed. If the state average is five percent of days billed are denied by the review organization, then that five percent is the baseline for length of stay patterning.

If a facility has 250 admissions in a six-month period for a total of 1750 days and 123 days were determined to be unnecessary by the physician-reviewers, this would be a pattern. A utilization pattern, whether for length of stay or admissions, requires a corrective action plan.

A corrective action plan requires a systematic plan to reduce the number of unnecessary admissions or prolonged length of stay that results in denied days. The plan must address the reasons for the denials, education for staff and physicians plus internal monitoring to identify problem areas before a new pattern develops.

At some review organizations, the facility may challenge admissions or denied days on the list and try to have them removed from the counted days or admissions. A facility may question inclusion on the list of a court ordered stay, as they had no control over the admission and could not refuse to admit the patient, even though the patient did not meet criteria for admission.

Another frequent reason to question a case is a missed successful appeal. When the report was generated, a denial that was overturned during the appeals process may not have been data entered in time to subtract that admission from the list. A case can also be overlooked or a data entry error be made.

Any facility that is notified of a confirmed utilization pattern should cross-reference all successful appeals to be sure those cases were removed prior to the confirmation of a pattern. Deadlines from various departments within the PRO may be different and cases can in limbo during the profiling period for a utilization pattern.

After a pattern is identified, a panel of physicians will evaluate the corrective action plan submitted by the hospital for appropriate interventions to prevent another utilization pattern. If the panel decides the facility's corrective action plan is insufficient, they may revise the plan and require compliance for the new interventions on the part of the facility.

At the end of the six-month monitoring period, the panel will evaluate the facility's compliance and whether the interventions did reduce the number of denied admissions or denied days. If the facility has not reduced the percentage of denials, the facility may have to modify the corrective action plan and resume monitoring for another six to twelve months. The panel of physician-reviewers may develop the new corrective action plan or development may be the responsibility of the hospital.

The government program is notified of the failure to improve and the extension of the corrective action plan. A facility that is in a corrective action plan for a utilization pattern for more than a year may require intensive intervention on the part of the state, government agency or Peer Review Organization.

If the panel sees sufficient improvement in the percentage of denials, the corrective action plan is terminated and the government program is notified. No other action will be necessary by the facility, unless they fall into another pattern in the future.

Each time a pattern is identified, the hospital will be responsible for a corrective action plan. A previous plan may be modified and used for a new utilization pattern or a new plan can be developed. Unfortunately, many hospitals fall in and out of utilization patterns.

CHAPTER FOUR

▼

QUALITY OF CARE REVIEWS

Katie's frantic parents brought her to the Memorial Hospital Emergency Department late one evening. Two year-old Katie was complaining of abdominal pain and having frequent episodes of vomiting. She was febrile and crying. Her parents brought her to Memorial when the acetaminophen the telephone triage nurse recommended failed to help her.

During the physical assessment in the ED, the following symptoms were noted in the medical record by the nurse and confirmed by the emergency medicine physician: mucus membranes dry, patient weak and fretful, no guarding or rebound, two episodes of vomiting for a total of 250cc, patient is febrile.

Orders included a normal saline drip to run at 35cc per hour, acetaminophen rectally for fever, draw electrolytes and admit to Pediatrics floor when bed is available.

The ED nurse initiated the IV, administered acetaminophen and called the report to the Peds nurse assigned to Katie. The lab was notified of the order for electrolytes and the phlebotomist was able to draw blood within the hour.

Soon after labs were drawn, Katie was transferred to the pediatric unit where she continued on IV fluids and vital signs were monitored every four hours. The pediatrician on call gave telephone orders: vital signs every four hours, clear liquid diet starting in the morning, I&O, repeat electrolytes in the morning and call results to the pediatrician when available.

In the morning, the phlebotomist rounded at 0530 and drew blood for the repeat electrolyte monitoring. Katie was able to go back to sleep after the blood draw. Change of shift occurred at 0700.

During report, the night shift nurse directed the oncoming nurse to call the lab results to Katie's pediatrician when available. Lab results for tests drawn at 0530 were generally available by 0900.

At 0815, the day nurse assessed Katie and noted her to be weak and fretful, refusing oral intake, no vomiting so far that shift and vital signs were unchanged. Katie was bathed by her mother and then went back to sleep.

At 1120, the day shift nurse completed all her morning assessments. At the nursing desk, she looked over all the lab reports for her patients, noting Katie's potassium level was 2.3, a panic low level. The nurse asked the unit secretary if the lab called the panic level to the floor. The unit secretary had not received any calls from the lab.

While she waited for the pediatrician to call back, the nurse noted the lab report was from the labs drawn the night before in the emergency department. The report from the morning labs had not yet arrived.

The nurse informed the pediatrician of the potassium level and accepted telephone orders for potassium supplements to be added to the IV fluids, repeat electrolyte level STAT and call results when available.

Katie responded well to treatment and her potassium level slowly returned to normal. Her vomiting did not return and she is discharged with orders to follow-up with the pediatrician in one week.

*   *   *

Unlike a malpractice lawsuit in which there must be damages or a bad outcome, when reviewing for quality of care concerns, it is the *risk* to the patient and not necessarily the outcome that determines a citation for a quality of care issue. In Katie's case, she did not experience any harmful consequences because of the missed low potassium level, appropriate care was initiated as soon as it was discovered and Katie made a full recovery.

In the review process, the nurse-reviewer would refer Katie's case to a reviewing pediatrician for a determination of whether or not Katie was placed at risk when the panic low potassium level was not noted for several hours. Unlike the utilization process, the facility and the physician are both involved in the process from the beginning.

A citation can be sent to a facility on behalf of employees. Employees are the nursing staff, pharmacists, emergency room physicians, radiologists or any other professional that is not in private practice. Citations are also sent directly to physicians that are independent of the facility. Admitting privileges are not an employment contract.

The physician-reviewer will review the medical record to determine if Katie was placed at risk during her hospital stay. Risk is categorized into three levels; minimal risk, moderate risk or significant risk. Should the pediatrician reviewing Katie's medical record determine she was placed at risk, the physician-reviewer must then decide what level of risk was involved and what alternative care was indicated.

A minimal risk is generally recognized as a documentation error that did not detrimentally impact on the care received by the patient. For example, the attending physician forgot to sign the comprehensive H&P completed on the day of admission. For minimal risk issues, no follow-up by the cited party may be necessary. It is an informational citation only.

For moderate risk issues, the patient was placed at risk for harm, but not at a level that is expected to cause permanent physical or mental impairment, life-threatening complications or death. A good example of a moderate risk issue is failure to follow up on an abnormal urinalysis in an otherwise healthy patient. A clean catch repeat of the lab is needed, but the patient is not at a significant risk for complications. If the repeat urinalysis was not ordered, a citation can result.

A significant risk issue is one where the patient could have, or was, seriously impaired, suffered life-threatening complications, maiming or death. An example of a significant risk issue would be where an IV pump was not properly set and an already compromised patient receives a one-liter bolus of fluid. A citation would depend on the status of the patient. Fluid overload would be a significant issue for an infant or CHF patient, but may not be for a twenty year old being treated for dehydration.

The physician-reviewer in Katie's case determines failure in the lab reporting system at Memorial Hospital placed Katie at significant risk for a cardiac event due to the delay in treating the hypokalemia. The alternative care is a timely notification to Katie's physician of the panic level potassium level to allow for timely intervention. The quality of care citation is issued to the hospital on behalf of the lab department and the nursing staff.

A second quality of care citation is issued to Memorial Hospital on behalf of the emergency room physician for failure to follow up on ordered labs. The reviewer determines Katie was placed at significant risk for a cardiac event and the alternative care is for the emergency room physician to follow up on ordered labs.

Quality concerns are cited to the pediatrician for failure to personally assess Katie after being informed of the panic level lab and failing to order cardiac monitoring until the electrolytes had stabilized. Both issues placed Katie at significant risk for inadequate intervention to prevent complications of hypokalemia. The alternative care would be for the pediatrician to assess Katie and order the cardiac monitoring until the potassium level had normalized.

The physician-reviewer sends the quality concern determination to the Medical Review Analyst responsible for processing quality of care citations. The nurse verifies all the information in the medical record and sends separate letters to Memorial Hospital and the treating pediatrician.

The hospital is only informed of the citations for the facility, the physician will only be notified of the issues specific to him or her.

All quality of care issues are kept confidential at this point in the review process. Any issues cited on behalf of hospital employees are sent to a representative at the hospital and not to the individual employee. Physician issues are sent to the physician's office and not the hospital.

In the letter to Memorial Hospital, the PRO nurse gives a brief history and then lists the quality concerns, risk to the patient and alternative care recommended by the physician-reviewer. The hospital has thirty days to respond to the issues. This is not optional. Failure to respond to the issues will result in an automatic confirmation of the concerns cited by the reviewer and the case will proceed to the final level of review.

The nurse sends the separate letter to the pediatrician, again only listing the concerns specific to the physician, risk to the patient and the alternative care recommended by the physician-reviewer. The pediatrician has thirty days to respond. Again, this is not optional.

The Memorial Hospital appeal level response notes the lab results were delayed, not lost. Katie suffered no ill effects and this was an unusual occurrence at the facility as a result of higher than expected admissions through the emergency department that night. The hospital noted their protocols do call for immediate notification to the physician in the event of a panic level lab finding and the lab personnel had been counseled on the incident. The hospital asserted that Katie was at most placed at a moderate risk from the delay.

In the physician's response, the pediatrician pointed out that immediate action was taken as soon as the notification of the lab result was received. Due to the supplementation and low probability for a patient of Katie's age to have complications from a short-lived drop in potassium, cardiac monitoring was not necessary.

The Medical Review Analyst adds the responses to the medical record and selects a physician-reviewer to perform a second level review. The medical record and responses are sent out to the second reviewer for a determination. The physician-reviewer at this stage of the review process may uphold the citations, reverse the issues, modify the citation and/or raise new issues.

In Katie's case, the second level physician-reviewer upholds all hospital issues raised at the first level of review. Katie was placed at significant risk for a cardiac event and the alternative care to the hospital is immediate notification to the physician of panic level labs and the emergency room physician to follow up on ordered labs.

For the pediatrician, the physician-reviewer downranks one issue to a moderate risk and uphold the other. The issue of cardiac monitoring is upheld as a significant risk to Katie, while the failure to personally assess Katie when informed of the hypokalemia is now at a moderate level.

Both cited parties are informed of the second level determination for their issues only. Confidentiality is still maintained at this point. The parties are given fifteen days to respond before the case proceeds to a panel of three physicians for final confirmation of the significant risk issues. This response is optional for all parties involved.

As both parties have already supplied all they information they have, neither elects to respond prior to a panel review. The three physician-reviewers meet via telephone conference to discuss Katie's case. Two reviewers are pediatricians and one is an emergency medicine physician.

After consideration of the medical record and additional information from the cited parties, the panel confirms the pediatrician issue of failing to order cardiac monitoring. The panel does not review quality issues that have been downranked at a previous level of review. Issues reduced to a lesser level of risk usually require no more action of any kind.

The panel confirms Katie was placed at significant risk for a missed complication of the hypokalemia with alternative care recommendations of ordering cardiac monitoring until the potassium level was normalized.

For the hospital, the panel confirms both issues. Katie was placed at significant risk for cardiac complications from the missed hypokalemia. The recommended alternative care is for the lab to notify the physician of the panic level lab and for the emergency room physician to follow up on any labs ordered.

At this point, confirmation of the hospital issues and the physician issue is sent to the hospital. This will be the first time Memorial Hospital is aware of the physician issue, unless the pediatrician had informed the hospital on his own. The pediatrician will be informed of the confirmation of his issue only.

Issues remain confidential until the last level of review to protect the parties until a confirmation of the quality issues is given. There is always a possibility the panel will decide there are no quality of care concerns that placed the patient at significant risk. There is no need for the hospital to know of the possibility of an issue until it is confirmed. This is to protect the treating physician until a panel determination is reached.

Now that a quality issue has gone through the entire quality review process and been confirmed, Memorial Hospital is required to implement a corrective action plan. The plan must address all the issues and contain a plan to prevent a future occurrence. The government program is informed of the confirmed issues, the identity of the cited parties and the corrective action plan requirement. The government program can elect to share this information with the licensing board for that state.

The prevention plan must include an education component for the staff and the treating physician. The plan must include monitoring of similar cases to prevent another issue of this nature. Typically, the hospital is required to submit proof of continuing education the physician received, the education of staff members and reports of internal monitoring for six to twelve months.

After the monitoring is completed, the same three physicians that confirmed the issues at panel level will reconvene to determine if the corrective action plan requirements have been met. If there are no further concerns of inadequate systems in place for prevention of similar issues, the corrective action plan is terminated and the government program is informed of the completion of the plan.

The Medicare Peer Review Organizations will also accept complaints regarding quality of care directly from the patients or families involved. The patient, family or other representative may call the PRO and ask to lodge a complaint against a physician, hospital, one-day surgery center or nursing home.

The compliant from the patient may also be submitted in writing. After the complaint is received from the patient or representative the review organization then conducts an investigation using the peer review model.

Medicaid review organizations may also conduct reviews of Medicaid managed care programs, nursing homes or other medical care providers. The peer review model is used, but variations are common due to the different nature of the various medical care settings.

Not all quality cases proceed through the entire process:

1. A hospital receives a letter of citation for poor quality of care. The treating physician ordered a series of PTTs for a patient on Heparin and the lab results are not in the medical record. The hospital's quality issue is failure to obtain labs as ordered by the physician. The physician may be cited for failure to ensure orders are carried out. When the hospital reviews the chart, the lab results are included in the record. The labs were not copied and sent in with the rest of the chart. On appeal, the hospital simply copies the lab results and submits them as evidence of orders carried out. The Peer Review Organization will then reverse the citation at this level.

2. A physician is cited for prescribing a medication that is listed on the patient's allergy alert list. A letter is sent to the physician outlining the quality citation. The physician responds with the rationale that the patient had expected side effects of nausea with the medication and it was not a true allergy. The second level

physician-reviewer upholds the citation with the rationale that the medication was listed as an allergy and the ordering physician should have chosen another medication or deleted the medication from the allergy list. At panel level, the three physician-reviewers determine the patient was not placed at significant risk. They decide the risk was moderate and no corrective action plan is necessary.

3. The nurse-reviewer screens a case and refers it to a physician-reviewer because the patient was in the emergency room for over six hours without pain medication being prescribed. The patient was admitted for angina controlled with nitroglycerin. The complaints of pain were for the headache that resulted from the nitroglycerin therapy. The physician-reviewer determines this was a moderate risk issue and the case is not pursued any further.

4. During the screening process, the nurse-reviewer questions the failure of the treating physician to attend treatment team meetings for a highly suicidal patient. The physician-reviewer cites the physician for a significant risk issue. The patient was placed at significant risk for continued suicidal behavior and a bad outcome without the input of the psychiatrist on the case. The physician responds that he was at the team meetings, but failed to sign the treatment plan. At second level, the physician reviewer downranks the issue to a minimal risk. No further action is required by any of the parties involved.

Facilities and physicians may be profiled for quality issue patterns. At the end of a profiling period, all the quality issues cited to a facility or physician are evaluated. The profile list may include all issues, all moderate risk issues or only the significant issues confirmed by the panel of physicians.

Let's assume a review organization looks at all the moderate level risk issues. The PRO is looking for a pattern of moderate level risk determinations for the same issue. Memorial Hospital has twenty-three moderate level risk issues for failure to follow physician orders. On the list are fourteen instances of frequent vital signs not obtained as ordered, six cases of labs not obtained as ordered and three cases in which the PRN medications were not given as ordered.

A pattern is determined to exist based on the number of moderate issue cases divided by the total number of cases billed by Memorial Hospital for this profiling period. In this case, twenty-three cases divided by the total cases of 124 shows that eighteen percent of Memorial's cases receive a moderate risk issue citation.

This is more than the six percent allowed by the rules of The Peer Review Organization. Therefore, Memorial Hospital has a quality of care pattern and must develop a corrective action plan similar to the one for a significant risk issue.

The panel of three physician-reviewers will evaluate the corrective action plan in the same manner as a significant quality issue. The plan will be monitored for six to twelve months. In effect, a pattern of moderate risk issues become a significant risk issue and follows the same procedures.

A facility may have several corrective action plans being monitored and never be cited for a significant quality of care deficiency. The rationale is that a pattern of substandard care, whether or not a patient was at significant risk, requires monitoring to improve patient outcomes and decrease extended hospital stays as a result of complications from the substandard care.

▼

CHAPTER FIVE

10 SIGNIFICANT QUALITY ISSUE EXAMPLES

The significant issues upheld by the review organizations span almost every medical specialty and can involve any hospital unit. The patient need only be placed at a significant risk for an issue to be confirmed at the final level of review.

No actual harm to the patient has to occur. In cases where the patient does suffer actual harm as the result of medical care, the cases are treated the same as the ones where only risk is involved.

1. A 19 year-old was involved in a one car motor vehicle accident requiring extraction from her vehicle. A passenger in the car was pronounced dead at the scene. In the emergency department, the patient was noted to have two compound ankle fractures with significant bleeding. Clamps were applied to stop the bleeding and an orthopedic surgeon was notified. The orthopedic surgeon and the physician on-call, in this case a general surgeon, examined the

patient and scheduled surgery for repair of the ankles by the orthopedic surgeon.

In the operating room, the patient developed hypotension and an irregular heart beat. The patient then coded on the operating table. After resuscitation, the general surgeon came into the operating room and began exploratory surgery of the chest and abdomen looking for missed internal injury. No injury was found. The patient again coded and could not be revived.

While reviewing all of the medical documents in the case, the Peer Review Organization found a radiology report in the medical record of a cardiac contusion and liver laceration. The x-ray had been ordered in the emergency room prior to the arrival of the orthopedic surgeon and the general surgeon. The emergency room physician, the orthopedic surgeon and the general surgeon had all missed the x-ray report.

2. A 47 year-old male was admitted to the psychiatric unit for command hallucinations telling him to kill his sister. The voices were telling him the devil lived in his sister's body and the only way to save her was to send her to heaven. Upon admission to the unit, the patient tried to hurt another patient that now had the devil living in her body. The patient required four point leather restraints for the safety of the unit.

Nine minutes after the staff left the restraint room; the patient began screaming that the devil was burning him alive. Staff entered the room and found his bed was on fire. The patient had not had a clothing and body search prior to being placed in restraints. The patient managed to reach into a pocket and get a contraband lighter.

The patient had then set his bed on fire with the lighter he had in his pocket since being admitted to the unit. The sprinkler system did activate and employees on the floor were able put out the fire. Two mental health technicians received minor burns to the face and hands. The entire psychiatric unit had to be evacuated. The patient died of his injuries.

The staff noted the evacuation of the unit, but did not document the reason for the evacuation. The patient's progress notes merely noted the patient was transferred to the emergency room where he expired from smoke inhalation. Requests for more information made by the PRO uncovered the cause of the patient's injuries.

3. A psychiatrist at a large urban facility admitted a 28 year-old for self-mutilating behavior. The patient cut her arms and legs multiple times to relieve inner tension and reduce her anxiety level. The psychiatrist completed a psychiatric evaluation within 24 hours of admission as required by standards of care. The psychiatrist did not see the patient again for 10 days. There were telephone orders and evidence of the nurses consulting with the psychiatrist during the telephone calls.

On the tenth day, the psychiatrist examined the patient prior to writing discharge orders. The patient attended groups and was supervised by the staff. The patient was stable for discharge, but the physician was cited for failing to demonstrate active involvement in the patient's care.

In medical cases, physicians must evaluate the patient every day. In psychiatric cases, the standard of care may be evaluations three, four or five times a week. Even though the psychiatrist is not required to assess the patient every day, frequent evaluation is the standard that is enforced by the review organizations. Failure by the treating psychiatrist to evaluate the patient frequently can also lead to denial of days during the stay.

The rationale for the payment denial is that if the patient was not acute enough to need frequent physician evaluation, the patient was not acute enough to require an inpatient stay. The patient could have been safely treated in a partial hospital or other intensive outpatient program and received the same degree of physician care.

4. A nine year old was admitted to the child/adolescent unit for out of control anger and physical aggression toward siblings. The patient had tied a scarf around his infant sister's neck and tried to choke her. On the second hospital day, the patient told a social worker at the hospital that his stepfather had inappropriate sexual contact with him. The social worker notified the patient's physician.

Social workers at the state's Child Protection Services were notified on the day of discharge, the seventh hospital day. Child Protection Services asked the child remain in the hospital until a preliminary investigation could be made and the patient's safety ensured at home. The patient had already been discharged from the unit when the call to the child abuse agency was made. The hospital and the treating physician were cited for failure to ensure a safe discharge for the patient and failure to notify child protection services in a timely manner.

The hospital responded that the policy at the facility was to wait until discharge to report abuse to lessen the animosity of the parents during the treatment process and prevent parents taking children out of the facility before they were stable enough for discharge for outpatient counseling. The issue was upheld at the panel level and the facility rewrote their child abuse reporting policy.

5. A 64 year-old female was admitted to the med-surg unit for treatment of pneumonia. During the admission, the patient told the nurse she was also having pain in her left breast and had discovered a lump that morning. The nurse noted the patient's complaint, but

did not inform the physician. The physician did not make any notation in the medical record of the reported breast pain or the presence of a lump in the left breast.

The patient did not receive any follow up on the complaint until eight months later when the Peer Review Organization cited both the hospital and the physician for the oversight. The patient was contacted as part of the corrective action plan required of the facility. The patient had not received any diagnostic testing or other treatment for the breast lump.

The patient indicated she thought there was no cause for concern, since the physician had not ordered a mammogram or other testing. Both the hospital and the physician were cited for placing the patient at significant risk for a missed cancer diagnosis and inadequate treatment.

6. A 36 year-old was admitted through the emergency department for alcohol withdrawal symptoms. The patient denied any history of drug use other than alcohol. The patient was complaining of sweats, tremors and weakness. There was no history of blackouts or DTs with previous attempts at detoxification. The emergency room nurse approached the patient to evaluate for impending DTs per the standard of care.

While she was in the examining room, a crisis occurred with another patient and she was called away. The nurse inadvertently left a Morphine filled syringe in the room that was intended for another patient. It was unclear if the syringe had fallen out of a pocket or was placed on a bedside table by the nurse.

The patient was able to self-inject the Morphine before the error was discovered. Although sedated, the patient did not suffer any long-term effects from the Morphine. The hospital was cited on behalf of the emergency room nurse for failure to ensure a safe environment for a patient with alcohol withdrawal and failure to properly handle controlled substances in the emergency department.

7. A patient on the psychiatric unit was being treated for bipolar disorder with mania. The psychiatrist ordered Lithium at a standard initiating dose. The patient refused blood draws to monitor the Lithium level for several days. Nursing staff noted the patient's refusal to have lab work completed. No telephone calls were made to inform the psychiatrist of the continued noncompliance with ordered testing. There were no notations in the physician progress notes of the lack of lab results in the medical record for the ordered Lithium levels.

   On the sixth hospital day, the patient was unsteady on his feet, had slurred speech and vomiting. A STAT Lithium level was obtained. The patient had Lithium toxicity and required transfer to an ICU.

   The hospital was cited for failure to notify the physician of the continued refusal for blood tests to check Lithium levels. The physician was cited for failure to follow up on the Lithium level orders.

8. A patient with a long history of cardiac artery disease was being monitored on the telemetry floor. The patient had a myocardial infarction and coded shortly after admission. Resuscitation efforts were initiated immediately by the telemetry nursing staff. A nurse on the unit was responsible for charting the actions taken during the code.

   The review organization cited the hospital due to a two-minute gap in code charting. The citation was for inadequate resuscitation efforts in compliance with ACLS standards. The hospital responded in appeal with a letter stating all step of the ACLS standard were followed, just not written down.

The citation was upheld at the panel level of review; as there was no way to determine if the proper actions were taken. The resuscitation efforts were unsuccessful. The panel indicated that the failure to resuscitate the patient did not have any bearing on the panel decision. The issue was the lack of documented intervention that placed the patient at risk. If the interventions had been documented, the issue would not have been raised.

9. A twenty-year old, with a history of one live birth and one spontaneous abortion, was admitted for a hysterectomy with oophorosalpingectomy. The diagnosis was fibroids with significant monthly bleeding and anemia. There was no documentation in the record of previous treatment with hormone therapy or other non-invasive treatment options.

   The patient had a low normal hemoglobin level. There were no indications in the medical record that the patient had lower hemoglobin levels in the past that had been treated with iron supplements or other intervention.

   The physician was cited for failing to try nonsurgical intervention prior to a hysterectomy in a young patient. The physician was also cited for removing the ovaries without medical indication for such removal. The physician responded that the procedure was suppose to be billed as an outpatient procedure, so the PRO did not have jurisdiction to cite a quality concern.

   No information was supplied to the review organization about previous treatment that occurred on an outpatient basis. The hospital was also cited for failing to monitor the operating room for unnecessary procedures.

   The hospital was unable to obtain any clinical records from the physician for a response. The case was billed as an inpatient stay and that cannot be changed once the review process has started.

The citations to both the physician and the hospital were confirmed at the panel level of review.

10.A patient was admitted with Major Depression and suicide ideation. The patient approached the nursing station at 0100 with a complaint of insomnia and increasing depressive thoughts. A mental health technician was at the desk and promised to pass on the complaint. There were no nurses at the nursing desk at the time of the complaint.

A mental health technician at the nursing station gave the patient relaxation tapes to listen to for the complaints of insomnia. There was no documentation in the medical record that the complaints were relayed to the nurse or other medical staff on the floor.

Forty-five minutes later the nurse began hourly bed checks on the floor. The patient was found hanging from the bathroom door. The patient has torn off a strip of the bedding to make a noose. The patient was resuscitated and transferred to the ICU.

The hospital was cited on behalf of the mental health technician for failure to relay the patient's complaint to the nursing staff in a timely manner. The hospital responded that they had fired the tech and no other incidents of this manner had ever occurred. The issue was upheld at the panel level.

CHAPTER SIX

FOCUSED-QUALITY STUDIES

Peer Review Organizations also conduct focused studies en masse of the care given to recipients with a specific diagnosis. Community-acquired pneumonia, asthma and Type II diabetes are the most popular areas of study at this time. Medicare has even developed the project-in-a-box program, to supply hospitals with all the materials and protocols necessary to duplicate the study for comparison with state or federal studies.

During a focused study, the review organization studies a targeted patient population to compare the care received as a whole against accepted standards of care. Guidelines are developed or chosen by a panel of experts that have agreed to participate in the study. Physicians do not have to be reviewers and other medical professionals, such as diabetes educators, respiratory therapists, and physical therapists are asked to participate.

For a Type II diabetes study at one review organization, the guidelines developed by the American Diabetes Association for preventative outpatient care were used to evaluate the Medicaid population. The panel considered guidelines from the American Medical Association, the American

Academy of Family Physicians and the Centers for Disease Control before deciding on the ADA standards.

Outpatient records were requested from individual physicians or clinics as part of the study. The cases were requested based on the coding information on the outpatient claim. Each patient's care over a one-year period of time was compared to the recommendations made by the ADA for glucose monitoring, microalbumin testing, HbA1C monitoring, retinal examinations and other indicators.

Since outpatient clinic records were needed for the study, physicians and clinics in the state were asked to participate on a voluntary basis. When inpatient hospital care is studied the records already available through the review processes are used. Outpatient studies are more difficult to conduct, in large part due to the lack of voluntary submission of clinic records. Physicians are asked to participate in many different studies by many different organizations and it is impossible for them to comply with every request.

Physicians also fear their clinic records will be reviewed for quality of care citations, which is not true. The Peer Review Organizations have limited areas where they may raise quality of care concerns based on the contract they signed with the government program.

The results of the diabetes care study, as a whole, was then reported to the state Medicaid agency with recommendations for areas of improvement. There are no quality of care citations made for focused studies and the individual medical care provider is not identified in any reports.

Each hospital and medical association in the state was given a copy of the report and the recommendations of the panel. A follow up study to measure improvements in the state was performed after one year. This report was then released to state providers.

Another PRO focused study looked at pediatric asthma care. The asthma panel worked closely with The Asthma Consortium and other organizations to recommend acute care interventions, primarily in the emergency departments throughout the state, to alleviate symptoms quickly and prevent recurring emergency visits for asthma control. A follow up study was scheduled to look at whether or not the recommendations were effective in promoting asthma control in children.

The focused quality studies are an important tool for evaluating preventative care and other services that do not routinely receive scrutiny. However, unless the studies are being used for increasing the quality of care in the United States, the government programs should look at whether or not the high cost of the studies is justified with reasonable improvements in care.

Some follow up studies have shown that no improvement resulted from the recommendations, that facilities do not read or follow the recommendations and that facilities sometimes do not even receive the information. These intensive studies are costly and should show improvement in care as a result or dropped in favor of an alternative method of quality improvement.

CHAPTER SEVEN

FOR THE STAFF NURSE

Consider the following progress note:

1510-pt was assessed q4, meds given, q4 hour monitoring to continue

This nurse was assessing the patient, giving medications, answering call lights, and probably giving various treatments. How is the patient doing after the nurse has given excellent care this shift? If someone had to rely solely on the documentation in the medical record, as a peer reviewer does, that question cannot be answered. There is no specific information about the patient in the progress note.

A medical record is not a timecard. It is a tool used by medical professionals to track the status of the patient and communicate the patient's progress with other members of the treatment team. That's why it's called a progress note. Any entries made by the nurse in the medical record are to communicate to others, including attorneys, juries and Peer Review Organizations, how the patient responded to intervention and monitoring.

Yes, there should be notations of the nurse's actions—in response to the patient's status. If the physician on-call is paged due to a patient's complaint of pain, that should be included in the medical record. So should the reason for calling, the orders received, the patient's response to intervention and any monitoring of pain performed.

The above progress note could have said:

1510-patient assessed q4, no c/o pain, VSS, neb tx given at 1300, slight crackle LUL,Dr. Doe assessed pt, no orders received, cont q4 hour assess.

How is the patient doing after receiving excellent nursing care this shift? The patient has no pain, vital signs are stable, and the patient received nebulizer treatments as ordered and continues to have slight crackles. The physician saw the patient and no other interventions were ordered. When asked about the patient in six months, this nurse could give information specific to the status of the patient.

When this case is reviewed by an outside organization, there will be information available to respond to any inquiries made during a review. Physician-reviewers do give weight to the documentation made by the nursing staff. If the nursing staff notes the patient is being monitored and no problems are noted, then the question of need for hospitalization will never come up.

Without information in the medical record by both the nurses and the physicians as to why the patient is there and what progress is being made, then why should a government program pay for what appears to be unnecessary hospital services? Monitoring the patient can be done by a home health nurse if the patient is stable, monitoring can even be done as a series of outpatient appointments if the patient is doing well.

Besides being patient-specific with charting, the staff nurse should be aware of the people reading the medical record and confusion that can result from unfamiliar abbreviations. With twelve patients, time is at a premium and charting is not a priority over patient care. However, effective charting does not mean more, but smarter documenting.

At one private psychiatric facility, the nursing staff noted the child/adolescent psychiatric patients were "cued per the HONOR system". There were no documents or checklists to let the reviewers know what this meant. Several quality citations were issues for the children being secluded more than once every twenty-four hours as regulated in the state's mental health code.

After several cases were referred to a physician-reviewer, it was discovered that the HONOR system was a behavior modification program, which is exempt from the seclusion rule. Many hours spent by the QA nurse at the facility could have been saved if the behavior modification program had been clearly documented.

If a patient is transferred to another unit, document the unit, not the floor number. An outsider does not know that 4th floor, East means an IMCU on the telemetry unit. Questions of appropriate transfer come up.

Nor does a reviewer know that a patient sent to "GC" (Good Choices) was transferred to an acute psychiatric unit. Medical and psychiatric services are billed differently and reviewed separately. Was this patient transferred to an outpatient clinic? There could be a quality concern raised if the patient were suicidal. Many hours by hospital QA/UR personnel would be wasted answering this question that would never come up if the nurse charted " pt to acute psych unit for suicide ideation."

After reviewing thousands of medical records, the most common examples of misunderstood or inadequate charting by physicians and staff nurses are:

1. Not making a notation that labs have been reviewed and do not require any follow-up. When looking at the labs that are slightly abnormal. It may seem obvious that no care is needed, so no notation is made. Physician-reviewers and nurse-reviewers want to know that if a lab is ordered, someone is following up on the order, even if results are normal. The rationale is that if there is not a system in place for follow-up on every lab ordered, an abnormal finding could be missed. If there is an order for an RPR and it is later discovered the patient was already seen at the

clinic—write it down. If a blood draw is canceled, note why it was not drawn.

2. The full name of the physicians treating the patient are not somewhere in the medical record. Yes, the nursing staff knows who Dr. M is, but the physician-reviewer does not and payment could be held up for weeks while it is figured out. Physicians are notified of admission and length of stay denials, even though their reimbursement is not in question. If the physician's name cannot be found, the case cannot be completed and payment is unnecessarily delayed. There are also instances where there are more than one " Dr. Humboldt" and the review organization spends days trying to find out which is the right one.

3. Writing "per protocol' without any information as to what protocol was followed. For example, a child adolescent psychiatric patient is "redirected per protocol" according to the medical record. This gives the impression the patient was redirectable and stabilizing. In fact, the nurse meant the child was redirected using all five steps of a behavior modification program used at the facility. This patient was not ready for discharge, yet the medical record read as if the patient was doing well. Six months later, the "redirected per protocol" entries were explained.

4. Documentation is optimistic, not realistic. At a facility in Illinois, the nursing staff did not want to put too many bad things in the medical record, because the psychiatric patients responded better to frequent praise. The patients were not reading the medical records, but praise in the chart became the norm. The facility had a high denial of payment rate and could not understand why. Objective, realistic charting is the goal, save the praise for the patient.

5. Writing vital signs down on a clipboard or other paper does not mean a thing if they do not make it into the medical record. It is very easy to get busy and forget to include the vital signs in the medical

record. It is very easy for a physician-reviewer to cite a quality issue for failure to follow physician orders for q2 hour vital signs, too. If assistant personnel are checking vital signs, it will still be the nursing staff that will be singled out in the quality citation.

6. If you do not document telling a patient not to get up without an assist and the patient falls, who does it appear is at fault? If you do not chart all the steps taken to prevent falls, such as siderails and bed alarms, then it was not done as far as the review organization is concerned. It is easy to forget all the things you routinely do for your patients, but when things go wrong, all of it needs to be in the medical record.

7. Never document things about co-workers or physicians in the medical record. Only document the events that occurred and save your commentary for the nurse manager or other supervisor. A mental health aide wrote in the medical record that the charge nurse was too busy making personal telephone calls again to see a suicidal patient. The tech also noted the charge nurse yelled and swore at him for bothering her. The tech checked on the patient who denied suicidal thoughts at that time. The patient never attempted to hurt himself, but the hospital was still questioned because of the notation in the chart. The hospital later replied in their letter of appeal that the charge nurse had been fired.

8. Late notes by nurses and physicians look like there is something to hide and the medical record will receive a very close reading. If you have to make a late entry, explain there a fire alarm, medical code or other reason for the delay. No explanation for a late entry may negatively influence the outcome of the review.

Every staff nurse working in a hospital will have his or her documentation reviewed at some point. It does not matter what hospital you work in or the type of patients you have. Medicare and Medicaid are the payment sources for a large percentage of the medical care received by hospitalized patients. Both programs review that care.

Nurses are responsible for a great deal of the care given to hospitalized patients and do a tremendous job with limited resources. Write it down in the medical record so everyone knows it.

If the peer review system is new to you, get more information from the QA/UR department at your facility. Find out what problems are being brought up by the PROs and what the expectations are for your facility. Is there a frequent problem with payment denials? Why are the claims denied? Is it because there is no information in the chart to support an admission or length of stay? Are there quality concerns for lack of follow up? Is follow up routinely charted?

The more information you have, the easier it will be to develop a charting style that is clear and unquestioned. Not only does this help your facility with the Peer Review Organizations; but also, two years from now if you are asked about a patient in a deposition for a lawsuit, you have clear documentation for a defense in the medical record.

CHAPTER EIGHT

▼

FOR THE UR/QA NURSE

When you accepted the position in QA/UR, did you have any idea you would spend so much time justifying care at your facility to a Peer Review Organization? There are so many different procedures for appeals, organizations to work with and medical records that need read. An inside look at the organization may be helpful.

If there is a sudden increase in the rate of referrals to physician-reviewers at your facility, first look to see if there were any changes made to standing orders or nursing forms. It takes time to learn new forms and the referrals are generally a problem with the new forms being used.

Stress completion of the new forms and the problems with leaving blanks when the case is reviewed. An incomplete medical record is responsible for delays in payment or outright denial of payment. This is preventable and an internal problem that should be addressed before high denial rates develop.

The majority of nurse-reviewers conducting an initial screening of a case are looking for a reason to approve a case, not refer it to a physician-reviewer.

Supply the reason for an approval in the medical record in an understandable manner and referrals will decrease. Educate the professionals that do the charting about what kind of problems are being found with charting and how to lessen the confusion.

Each government program has a handbook with rules and regulations that must be followed. Every facility approved by the program is given a copy of the handbook. If the answer cannot be found in the handbook, call the Peer Review Organization for assistance. Listen to the advice of the review nurse in charge of appeals or other review processes.

They know the system and have a better perspective of the physician-reviewers they work with. If they tell you nothing can be done to reverse a denial, they mean it. If they give advice on how to prevent future denials, they know what the physician-reviewers are thinking and are trying to help.

Not all physician-reviewers are created equal. Appeal every admission or length of stay denial. Each physician-reviewer has his or her own perspective on the case and the next level reviewer may have thinking more in line with your facility and/or be more willing to give the benefit of the doubt.

It is a sad fact that there are a few (thankfully, very few) physician-reviewers that may use personal prejudices to determine the outcome of a review. Board certification is not a guarantee of a good physician-reviewer.

Some physicians become reviewers because they sincerely want to make health care delivery in the United States better and more efficient. Others become reviewers because they want to tell others what to do. There are reviewers that have small private practices and do reviews to supplement their income. One reviewer called a PRO and asked for twenty reviews because he wanted to put a new deck on his vacation home. Whatever the motivation, they have the final say in a review.

Unfortunately, many appeals are based on the argument that the first level review was unfair. No additional information about the patient or medical rationale by the treating physician is included. If you base your appeal on this argument, you will lose. Appeal level physician-reviewers are looking for medical reasons for treatment, not an attack of the first level reviewer.

The physician reviewers do not know the criteria and arguing criteria with them is a waste of your time and opportunity to appeal. Concentrate on the patient care involved and accepted standards of care. That is what the physician-reviewers are looking at. Also, citing anti-dumping regulations as the reason for an inappropriate admission will not fly.

Even if the physician that provided the care is not involved in an appeal, discuss the case with him or her. They may have clinic notes that are helpful, a different angle to use in the appeal and they can provide the needed medical rationale to effectively defend the care given.

Many facilities handle all the appeals in the UR/QA Department without any input form the physicians that provided the care being questioned. Physicians are very busy, but without medical rationale from the physician, many appeals fail to convince a physician-reviewer of medical necessity of quality of care.

When handling an appeal, always send in written information, even if the appeal is done over the telephone. That way if there are any questions later about what was said during the telephone appeal, there is written information to refer to. Telephone appeals are not recorded and physician-reviewers can have memory problems, too.

The identity of the physician-reviewers is kept confidential for very good reasons. One physician-reviewer gave his name and telephone number during a telephone conference and was harassed by the cited physician for weeks after the citation letter was sent.

Another physician-reviewer gave his name, but not his telephone number during a conference. The cited physician was able to locate him through an Internet search. There are strong emotions attached to quality citations and the physician-reviewers are protected to keep them as reviewers.

If there is a complaint about a physician-reviewer, the PRO has procedures to follow. The Peer Review Organization is aware that some physician-reviewers are not the best reviewers on the roster and that not all
physician-reviewers communicate effectively over the telephone. Call the
PRO and ask for the person in charge of complaints. An investigation by
the PRO can be very successful for the cited party.

Remember that risk, not outcome, is the basis for the quality of care
citation. The patient may not have any adverse effects at all, but if there is
a risk that could have had a significant impact on the health of the patient,
an issue can be cited. This is not a lawsuit where damages must be proven.
It is peer review. The appeal should address the standards of care and not
the fact that the patient was not harmed.

One facility appealed a quality issue saying any action by a medical professional can create risk. The basis for a citation should be actual harm,
not what could happen. That may or may not be true, but the government
program sets the rules for quality of care citations and the physician and
nurse-reviewers follow the guidelines established by Medicare or
Medicaid. This is not an effective appeal, but the concern can be brought
up directly with the government program through the Centers for
Medicare and Medicaid (formerly HCFA).

If the appeals fail and your facility must develop a corrective action
plan, do not miss deadlines. If a plan is not submitted by the facility, the
physician-reviewers will develop one for the facility. The PRO developed
plan must be adhered to and may be much tougher to implement and
monitor than one developed internally by personnel familiar with practices and procedures already in place.

If it appears a deadline will be missed, call the review organization and
work out an extension. It may take a little effort to get an extension, but it
will be worth it to have your own corrective action plan in place. Many
facilities are not aware of extensions and exceptions being made by The
Peer Review Organizations.

One last piece of advice, reimbursement can take months. Do not add to the time by delaying the billing of a claim. Yes, you have one year after the date of discharge to bill, but why delay it? Most hospitals are not in a financial position to wait so long for reimbursement.

Some facilities bill months after a hospital stay and then must wait months for a review to be completed. Your facility should not have to wait any longer than necessary. Do the paperwork as early as possible. This also allows time if a mistake is made in billing or a bill is sent to the wrong agency. If you wait until the last minute and a mistake is made, you may not have the option of rebilling because of missed deadlines.

▼

CHAPTER NINE

25 OBSERVATIONS

1. Physicians—the nurses working in the PRO office handling your case do not care how many degrees or board certifications you have. They care about the information in the medical record. If your credentials are the only information you provide for an appeal, expect to lose. The additional information you send in the Peer Review Organization should be about the patient, what care was given and why. Your appeal should not be about yourself.

   Nurses handling appeals for physicians should not fall into the habit of praising the physician and not providing the patient information that is being requested by the review organization. The reviewers know most physicians operate under the highest quality standards, but there are questions being raised about this one patient. Concentrate on supplying the information that is specific to the patient and the case under review.

2. Most physician license numbers can now be found on the Internet. There is no reason to refuse to give it to the PRO nurse. Refusal to give information needed to complete a case will only delay payment. If your facility has a policy that physician license numbers cannot be given over the telephone, make sure the PRO has a directory of the physicians that practice at your facility, their mailing addresses and license numbers.

   If the nurses at the review organization cannot get the information any other way, they will have to hold the case until someone at the facility is willing to give out the information needed to complete the review process. Holding up payment for a month while waiting for a hospital employee to verify that Dr. X is indeed the admitting physician and Dr. Y only wrote the discharge orders can and does happen.

3. Cases involving exceptionally poor quality of care are rare. Most questions regarding care come up because the medical records are incomplete, poor handwriting by the professionals or contradictory statements among the medical team. Everyone on the treatment team should be aware of what is being written in the medical record. Everyone should be able to read what others are writing. Computerized charting has helped with this somewhat, but there are some terrible typos being entered into computerized charts.

   Facilities could save thousands of dollars in wasted utilization and quality department employee hours if there were standards for charting and the standards are enforced for both the nursing staff and the physicians. Physician handwriting may be an old joke, but it could be costing facilities thousands of dollars every year. That is not funny.

4. The inability of a facility to find placement for a patient after discharge is responsible for millions of dollars in wasted medical resources. If the federal government wants to reduce the budget for

health care services, they should be looking at the lack of adequate outpatient resources in many areas of the country.

Children and adults are being kept in the hospital for weeks until a nursing home or residential treatment program can be found to accept the patients. Lack of placement does not meet criteria for acute services and hospitals are not being reimbursed at an acute care rate for placement issues outside their control.

Some facilities are being reimbursed at an outpatient rate that may be less than $100 a day for care that costs $1000 a day. Other facilities may not receive any payment at all while they house a patient that cannot be placed in an appropriate residential facility.

5. Observation status is a cost-cutting measure, not a level of care and should be eliminated. If the government programs do not want to pay for these admissions, they should include it in the criteria. It is also unfair that a case denied a formal admission, with a recommendation for observation status instead, cannot be rebilled as an observation stay so that the facility may receive some reimbursement.

   In Illinois, the hospital may not rebill a claim to Medicaid that is denied acute care reimbursement, even if the physician-reviewer agrees the patient required hospital care, but only at an observation status level. So if the reviewer says the patient was acute enough for an observation status hospital admission, but the claim was billed as an acute inpatient admission, the hospital does not receive any payment and cannot rebill the claim as an observation stay. A closer look at observation status is long overdue. Medicaid programs are paying observation status reimbursement for patients in ICU and other high acuity settings. That is not what observation status was intended for. It has created many problems and few solutions.

6. There are shortages of peer reviewers in some specialties, especially neurology, physical medicine, child/adolescent psychiatry and neu-

rosurgery. This results in less than ideal physician-reviewer matches or reliance on one or two specialists for most of the reviews.

Without a broad base of knowledge to draw on in the review process, reviews can become personal opinion and not based on medical judgment. In other cases, long delays in the review process occur because there are no specialists available to do the reviews. This delays payment and the entire process for the hospital and other cited parties.

7. If the psychiatric patient is stable enough to leave the hospital on pass without staff supervision, then the patent is stable enough to be discharged when they return from a successful pass. Short stays do not allow for multiple successful passes prior to discharging the patient.

Evaluate the pass policy and your facility and analyze how many length of stay denials are the result of a successful pass that is not followed with a discharge order. It has not been that long ago that the average stay for a psychiatric patient was thirty days. The average stay is now less than a week in many facilities. Reviewing physicians are well aware of the decrease and are not sympathetic to long stays for multiple passes and evaluation of functioning off the grounds. Partial hospital programs are being used for evaluation at home on a limited basis.

8. When a patient refuses to leave the hospital after being discharged by the physician, call the government program. They have procedures in place, and of course paperwork to be filled out, when this occurs. The patient is generally responsible for any charges after the physician signs the discharge order, unless the patient can prove they are not stable for discharge.

However, there is a catch. Many of the recipients of the government programs will not be able to pay for charges that accrue after the discharge order is ignored. The goal is for the patient to leave voluntarily when confronted with a potential bill for services.

9. The friendliest person on the telephone is only as good as the information given. Not every employee at the PRO office can answer every question. If you have a favorite person you like to deal with, make sure the information is as good as the personality. Developing a professional relationship with the nurses at the review organization can help facilitate problem solving at your facility. Hospitals that play one review nurse against another may be surprised at the result.

10. After a physician-reviewer has attended a seminar on any subject, he or she will invariably want to cite multiple quality issues on every case reviewed. This generally lasts two to three months. Physician-reviewers must provide medical rationale for every citation, so this decreases the chances of citations due to "post-seminar syndrome" going through.

   The nurses in charge of appeals and quality issues work very closely with the physicians to ensure accurate and even reviews. They may not have the final word on review, but they pick the physician-reviewers and analyze every part of the review. Physician-reviewers that cause frequent problems or turn in poor reviews are simply not picked to do any other reviews.

11. The government programs need to get together to develop one set of criteria and one set of procedures. Many program requirements are contradictory to the requirements of other programs. A state Medicaid program will require a set of procedures that is forbidden by the Federal Medicare program. So elderly patients that are being served by both government programs cause many internal billing and treatment problems for the medical care providers.

   If one set of criteria could be approved, it would be easier for medical providers to comply with the rules, cheaper for the government to oversee compliance and cheaper for the taxpayers that have to pay for all these programs.

12. Every case has a different flavor. Advice given by a PRO nurse for one case does not necessarily apply to another with the same diagnosis. There are overall rules for cases, but specifics are case sensitive. If the PRO nurse advises observation status billing for one patient, that does not mean every patient with the same principal diagnosis should be billed as observation. If there is an admission denial for a patient admitted for abdominal pain, rule out pancreatitis that does not mean every patient admitted for abdominal pain where pancreatitis is ruled out will be denied. It is patient-specific, unless addressed in the criteria.

There are lists of procedures that must be billed as outpatient procedures, known by names such as the Ambulatory Procedure List. Any patient undergoing a procedure on this list must be an ambulatory patient unless they have another condition or complication that requires admission. There are thousands of procedures on these lists.

13. Peer review employees are not "out to get you." If they were out to get you, they would be out of a job. Every determination is reported to the government program and complaints are looked at very closely. Not only does the PRO do an internal investigation of every formal complaint, but the government program may also be involved in the investigation. The review organization employees are trying to be fair and impartial in every review.

In most cases, the nurses try to gather as much information as is needed to reverse issues or approve payment. It is only in the cases of obvious medical error or dangerous hospital procedures where the nurses may look for information to uphold a significant quality issue.

14. As representatives of the government program, review employees are protected from lawsuits. Threatening the nurses with legal action after an adverse decision will not help your appeal and the physician-reviewers have the final say on any determination. Concentrate

on the status of the patient in any appeal, not emotional reactions to the decisions of the physician-reviewer.

The most successful appeals contain objective medical rationale for treatment decisions. Most emotional appeals fail. While a quality citation is a very emotional experience for the person cited, the same is not true for the physician-reviewer or review staff. For them, it is a routine citation and not unlike the hundreds of other citations they send out every year.

15. If you have a DRG coding question, the coding specialist, not the nurse-reviewer, is the best person to ask. The nurse-reviewer will decide whether the coding is accurate during screening, but the coding specialist is the one that must adhere to coding guidelines and works with the physician-reviewers on coding questions. If you want to save being put on hold or having your call transferred, ask for the DRG specialist in the beginning.

It is helpful if the person responsible for coding at your facility make the call, instead of the nurse or other personnel handling the appeal. Coders speak in another language, just as physicians and nurses do. A coding professional to coding professional telephone conference is much more effective.

16. An excellent clinician is not always an excellent physician-reviewer. They can do it, but have trouble conveying it to others or allowing for variations within standards of care. On the other hand, a physician-reviewer for one PRO had been cited for quality of care issues prior to becoming a reviewer. He was an excellent reviewer and quickly became a favorite choice for difficult cases in his specialty.

In that instance, the reviewer was better at the academics of medicine than at the practice of it. Physician-reviewers have biases just like everyone else. Arguing about it is pointless. Argue the treatment, argue acuity, and even argue the timing of the care, but "calling it like you see it" means your hospital will not get paid or the citation will stand.

17. Analyze the denials at your facility every six months before the semi-annual reports are released by the Peer Review Organization. If there are discrepancies between what your numbers say and what the PRO is reporting, when the reports are issued is the best time to bring it to the attention of the review organization. Waiting until the report is a year old to question an entry will result in much more time being required for the issue to be resolved.

18. Placement issues that are outside the control of the hospital and delay discharge are excluded from utilization reporting. All other place-ment issues are fair game. If your facility is in the habit of not con-firming placement and travel arrangements on the day before discharge, that is in the control of the hospital. If you rely on other agencies to arrange and confirm placement and do not contact them until very late in the hospital stay, that is within your control. If you wait until the day before discharge to report possible child abuse charges, not only is it a quality of care issue, but if discharge is delayed that is an over-utilization issue within your control.

19. On-site nurse-review screenings are faster than off-site reviews. If you have a large number of cases selected for review, check with the government program or the PRO about getting on-site reviews. This also gives your facility the opportunity to discuss the referred cases with the nurse-reviewer while she is at your facility.

With an off-site review, there is no opportunity for personal contact and asking questions at the time for the review while all the information is still fresh in her memory. They can be very helpful. Do not let them just drop off the cases that are being referred to a reviewing physician. Ask about what they are seeing and why they are referring cases. This will give you more time to prepare a defense of the case or make changes in internal processes to prevent future referrals.

20. Physician should discuss all quality issues with the facility before the hospital is informed by the review organization. If the facility has also been cited for the issue, it does not look good when the two responses contradict each other. It appears to be just passing the blame. It is better that both cited parties on the case work together and present a unified appeal. It will also give the facility a chance to gather information and other data in the event a corrective action plan is required.

21. The nurses in the office discuss quality issues with each other, but they are not going to discuss it with you, unless you are the cited party. Confidentiality of issues is an important aspect of their processes. The PRO employees sign confidentiality agreements and the review organization takes the issue of confidentiality very seriously.

Many office nurses handle the letters of appeal for the physician, but unless specifically granted permission by the physician, the review organization cannot discuss the case with the physician's office nurse. Although this does create difficulties for the physician that has turned over the appeal to his nurse, it also protects the physician that has not told his hospital of the citation.

22. One facility was having problems with mail delivery within the hospital and wanted the PRO to solve the problem by granting exceptions to the deadline for responses to utilization issues. The extension would give the mail a chance to catch up with the appropriate personnel. Internal problems need internal solutions. The facility was very frustrated by the lack of accommodation and continued to miss deadlines. This resulted in no appeal being performed for the late cases and an unknown financial loss as a result.

23. Calling the review organization for the status of the claim or sending a list of fifty cases to be looked up because you lost the paperwork will not endear you to the review organization staff. They work on tight deadlines, too. The nurses will look up the cases for you and send copies of letters, but it will be at their convenience, not yours. You may receive the paperwork too late to conduct an appeal or answer a quality citation. Frequently lost paperwork is a sign of a breakdown in an internal system and needs to be addressed quickly. Waiting for audit time is too late.

24. There were fewer coding problems when physicians were required to sign the attestation form. The attestation form is a cover sheet in the medical record listing all the diagnosis and procedures codes. The coding specialist that completes the coding for that particular chart signs the attestation form. In the past, after being coded, the physician looked over the coding sheet and then signed it in agreement with the codes listed. They "attested" to the accuracy of the coding. Coding specialists would like to see that practice revived. If your facility has frequent referrals for coding problems, consider incorporating physicians into your coding procedures. Use the resources you have and referrals will decrease. Frequent coding changes can trigger an audit or result in lost revenue.

25. The review organization nurses and physicians receive ongoing education. They have seminars, educational meetings and guest speakers. Offer to speak at one of their education meetings. This gives you a chance to outline why things are done certain ways at your facility, standards of care used by your staff and to ask questions of the review organization employees. Personal contact makes working together easier when the voice on the telephone becomes a real person. It may also give you the names of resources with the review organization to call when a question arises.

CHAPTER TEN

▼

WORKING FOR A
PEER REVIEW ORGANIZATION

For nurses looking for a change from the hospital or clinic environment, working for a Peer Review Organization is an option that will use the nursing skills you have acquired, as well as, increase your knowledge in multiple areas of medical practice and healthcare administration. Government regulations, health codes, research and medical care analysis are a big part of working within the review organization.

The Peer Review Organizations are looking for registered nurses with a solid clinical background and the desire to learn new ways of looking at healthcare. Nurses with a background in quality assurance or utilization management are in demand. Clinical backgrounds that are in demand include critical care and medical-surgical nursing.

There are numerous areas within the review organizations where a nurse or other medical professional can contribute their expertise. At the Illinois Medicaid PRO, the majority of the employees are nurses. Most of the nurses have years of clinical experience and at least a bachelor's degree. Masters prepared nurses are common.

Nurses may be employed in management positions or as reviewers. At one PRO, the CEO, COO and all of the upper management in charge of medical care analysis are nurses. Nurses are also managers in areas of statistical analysis and physician education.

The first year as a reviewer is a lot like the first year out of school. You will learn more about medicine and accepted practices in every specialty than you could ever imagine. You will develop working relationships with the physician-reviewers and you will learn to use English and not medical terms when corresponding with hospitals.

It is not all denials, medical errors and letter writing. While employed at a PRO, I worked on a statewide diabetes study, was a member of a team that researched and implemented a new telephone system, and trained new employees in quality assurance and utilization review procedures.

Working closely with every hospital in the state and over two hundred physician-reviewers can have a lighter side. Physician-reviewers may never see you face-to-face, but after years of talking over cases on the telephone they feel they know you.

In the case of one psychiatrist, after a difficult case was discussed he began asking me strange questions about my working style and education. He then "diagnosed" me as a Type A personality and suggested I take up his hobby. He rides his bicycle across the United States, usually 20 to 25 miles a day while on vacation.

One physician, with a name that rhymes with hitter, would not return a PRO nurse's telephone calls. She needed to clarify an issue he raised in a review and had no luck getting in contact with him for several days. While waiting to leave him another message on his voice mail, and probably thinking bad thoughts, she inadvertently asked that Dr. Shitter call her back as soon as possible. He returned her call within an hour.

Giving the benefit of the doubt is the policy at the PRO where I worked. All of the nurses would bring this up on occasion as a way of getting a difficult reviewer to drop or downrank an issue that really did not place the patient at significant risk.

One treating physician had apparently forged progress notes after being cited for lack of participation in his patient's medical care. The physician-reviewer knew it and the PRO nurse knew it, but the manager questioned whether we could prove it. There was some doubt about proving it.

The PRO nurse called the physician-reviewer (a psychiatrist) and raised the benefit of the doubt policy. The physician-reviewer replied, "You better come to my office right away. You need treatment for that delusional disorder if you think there is any room for doubt in this case." The issue stood, but was reversed at the panel level, which did give benefit of the doubt.

Another physician went a bit far with the benefit of the doubt policy. A treating physician discharged a patient that was not medically stable. The first physician-reviewer cited the treating physician for failure to stabilize the patient prior to discharge. The second level physician-reviewer reversed the issue. His rationale was there is always a possibility of a patient suffering complications of some kind after a hospital discharge. He gave the example of a patient being discharged and then being kidnapped by aliens in the parking lot, a serious complication to his recovery. The case was sent to another second level reviewer who upheld the issue and sent it to the panel level.

One new physician-reviewer called me while reviewing his first case on his own. He was having trouble reading the progress notes of the nursing staff. I asked him to fax the page in question to me and I would try to decipher it. What he faxed me what a page of computer language. The hospital used computerized charting and the physician-reviewer was trying to read the printout that showed how often the medical record had been accessed from the main server.

One treating physician, cited for a medical error, had his attorney call me and ask for more information about the citation. I explained that all the information was confidential and I could only release that information to the physician. Five minutes later, the same voice on the telephone identified himself as the treating physician.

I asked him to make his request in writing and I would send the information to his clinic office. Again, five minutes later, the same voice on the telephone called as asked the information be faxed to his clinic office and gave me a fax number to use.

The fax number had a different area code than his clinic telephone number. I called the clinic office and asked to speak with the treating physician to verify the fax number. The treating physician had a thick southern accent, which the "physician" on the telephone did not have. I agreed to send the information to the fax number Dr. Southern Accent gave me on the telephone.

Not only are the people interesting to work with, there are medical cases that can stretch even the physicians working on the case. In one case, a three year old died in a hospital from complications of a rare disease that caused massive sodium wasting diarrhea. I had never heard of the disease and could not find any information on it. The physician-reviewer had never heard of it either.

After extensive research that took weeks to complete, it was discovered that only ten people in the United States had ever been diagnosed with this condition and less than 100 worldwide. All of the children that had been diagnosed with the condition had died early in childhood. Determining the best course of treatment was left up to the treating physicians because of the lack of research into the condition.

The citation to the treating physician was reversed. There really were no standards of care to go by and the physician had treated the patient with accepted practices for other forms of diarrhea. The treating physician understood our dilemma and shared his research notes he kept on this patient.

TOVA is a controversial test for attention deficit hyperactive disorder. A treating psychiatrist used the test routinely for all patients suspected of having ADHD. The physician-reviewer questioned whether this testing was appropriate and whether or not Medicaid should pay for an expensive test that has not been widely accepted as reliable in diagnosing ADHD.

The PRO nurse involved in the case was not familiar with TOVA testing and asked the physician-reviewer to send any research she had on the subject to the office so all the PRO nurses could study it. At this point only one treating physician was billing for TOVA testing. The physician-reviewer sent over 150 pages of information, both for and against the use of TOVA testing.

Munchausen Syndrome is a rare mental illness in which patients induce illness and injury in order to seek medical attention and sympathy. Many patients with this condition become very conversant in medical terms and will shop around for physicians that will give them the treatment they want. In many cases, the treatment of choice for the Munchausen patient is surgical. They have medical histories that include multiple exploratory surgeries or surgical treatments for multiple illnesses.

A thick medical record came across my desk one afternoon. The patient was twenty-two and had the past medical history of a chronically ill eighty year old. She had surgery to remove her gallbladder, appendix, and spleen. She had had exploratory surgeries for abdominal pain and guarding behavior on exam. Her eyesight was poor from frequent infections and she had had surgery on her knees and wrists for unrelieved pain.

She had sought treatment this time for complaints of crippling menstrual pain and excessive bleeding. She refused any interventions except for a hysterectomy. The treating physician did not perform a hysterectomy, but did keep the patient in the hospital for three days for various testing. The nurse-reviewer questioned whether this testing required an acute care admission.

During the utilization review, the physician-reviewer suspected Munchausen Syndrome and approved the admission as a safety measure to prevent the patient from self-inflicting more harm that could result in dangerous consequences. Two months later, the patient's chart was again on my desk, this time a quality concern had been raised for an unnecessary hysterectomy in a young patient that had not receive non-surgical intervention prior to proceeding with the hysterectomy. The patient was admitted through the emergency room of another hospital with vaginal hemorrhaging. The quality citation was reversed.

A patient with a history of schizophrenia was admitted to Chicago area hospitals for a total of 235 days in a one-year period. The patient would be discharged from one hospital and then walk to another hospital and claim to be suicidal. The patient never gave the same history or reported taking the same medication at any of the hospitals.

After being discharged from one hospital with discharge medications of Paxil and Xanax he would tell the next hospital he was taking Trazadone and Valium. Because the patient was never on the medication for very long, he had minimal response to the drugs and there was a chance of drug interactions causing several complications.

When a review is conducted, only the hospital stay in question can be used to make a determination. Past hospital stays or citations cannot be sent to the physician-reviewer. The only reason this pattern of behavior was recognized was due to the patient having an unusual last name that the PRO nurse recognized. After so many admissions in a short period of time, the nurse was very familiar with the pattern and wrote a report of her findings for the manager of the department.

Unfortunately, the Illinois Medicaid system does not have any procedures in place to intercede when this type of behavior is discovered. The patient continued to be admitted to the hospital several times a month. In one given month, the patient was out of the hospital for a total of 72 hours.

After this case came to light, a PRO nurse did some digging into the cases in storage and found dozens of patients with this same pattern of behavior. In one of the cases, a 32 year old woman with a history of Major Depression would show up at the emergency room at a rural hospital two or three times a month asking for admission. She usually had minor self-inflicted cuts on her arms.

She lived alone and at one point admitted to a nurse on the mental health unit that she would get very lonely. When the loneliness became too much, she cut her arm and came to the hospital for admission so she could be around people for a while.

At one hospital, it was the treating physician's pattern of behavior that was the issue. The treating physician was in charge of a detoxification unit at a medium size urban hospital. During a one-month period, he admitted over 200 people for detox. The admission ranged from three to four days each. The detox unit has less than twenty beds and he is the only treating physician for that unit.

After looking at a profiling report, the questions were raised. How could a physician see this many hospitalized patients every day without weekend relief coverage and less than twenty beds? Spending only ten minutes with each patient during rounds equals 180 minutes or three hours, plus charting and any verbal reports from the nursing staff. The physician also had a clinic from which he was admitted many of the patients. At no time was there a progress note from another physician who was covering for a day off or vacation.

When questioned, the admitting physician admitted he was very close to burnout and was looking at new positions around the country. He had no idea when he took over a practice from another physician that he would go for months without a day off and spend between 10 and 12 hours a day just seeing patients. The physician was looking into going back to school and specializing in dermatology.

Another treating physician was cited numerous times a month for lack of participation in his patients' care. Letter after letter was sent and he failed to respond to most of them. His office was called almost on a daily basis asking for responses or information. He never took any of our calls and the only person we ever spoke to was his office manager.

Just when we were beginning to make jokes about the "phantom physician" practicing in our state, he personally requested a telephone conference with a physician-reviewer. The conference was set up and then disaster struck. The physician-reviewer ran into the treating physician at a conference shortly thereafter. Not only did the physician-reviewer confront the physician in public, she also accused his wife, a malpractice attorney, of legal malpractice.

Then the physician-reviewer called the office and told us all about the confrontation. She was quite proud of herself, but had to be dropped as a reviewer for her actions. The treating physician never called to complain and the incident was reported to management.

▼

CHAPTER ELEVEN

CONTACT INFORMATION

To have more effective interactions with the Peer Review Organization providing oversight of the care given in your facility, it is important to know what processes are used and the expectations required of each medical care provider. You would not perform a procedure on a patient without knowing how and why it is being done.

The same is true for the peer review system. Know what is being done by the review organization and why it is done that way. Find out what criteria is used by the review organization. Know what part you play in the process and what is expected from you by your facility and by the review organization.

Whether you are looking for employment opportunities or information you can use to learn more about the PRO and the expectations for your facility or practice, you can use the contact information below to get more information for the PRO in your area:

The Centers for Medicare and Medicaid (formerly the Health Care
Finance Administration aka HCFA)
7500 Security Blvd.
Baltimore, Maryland 21244
410-786-3000
www.hcfa.gov

If you would like to contact me, I can be reached at Raymond
Healthcare Consulting, P.O. Box 287, Sidney, IL 61877, or by e-mail at
lrraymond@yahoo.com. I would be happy to hear from you.

Below is a list of Peer Review Organizations and their contact information. Websites are listed where you can find more information about the
organization or you can contact the review organization directly with
questions.

Notice that several review organizations hold the contract for more
than one state or area and most hold the contracts for both Medicare and
Medicaid in that area or state.

The majority of the review organizations are not-for-profit organizations, but may have for-profit subsidiaries that contract with private com-
panies for third party external review, pre-certification of medical care or
case management services. The not-for-profit arm of the organization
contracts only with government agencies.

State	Peer Review Organization
Alabama	Alabama Quality Assurance Foundation One Perimeter Park South Suite 200 North Birmingham, Alabama 35243 Tel- 205-970-1600 www.aqaf.com
Alaska	PRO-West 721 Sesame Street, Suite 1A Anchorage, Alaska 98133 Tel- 907-562-2252 www.pro-west.com
Arizona	Health Services Advisory Group 301 E. Bethany Home road, Suite 157-B Phoenix, Arizona 85012 Tel-602-264-6382 www.hsag.com
Arkansas	Arkansas Foundation for Medical Care, Inc. 2201 Brooken Hill Drive Fort Smith, Arkansas 72908 Tel-501-649-8501
California	California Medical Review, Inc. One Sansome Street, Suite 600 San Francisco, California 94104 Tel-415-677-2000 www.cmri-ca.org
Colorado	Colorado Foundation for Medical Care 2821 South Parker Road Pavilion Towers II, Suite 605 Aurora, Colorado 80014 303-695-3300 www.cfmc.org

Connecticut

Qualidigm
100 Roscommon Drive, Suite 200
Middletown, Connecticut 06457
860-632-2008
www.qualidigm.org

Delaware

West Virginia Medical Institute
Independence Mall, Suite 56-58
1601 Concorde Pike
Wilmington Delaware 19803
302-655-3077
www.qualityinsights.org

District of Columbia

Delmarva Foundation for Medical Care, Inc.
1620 L Street NW, Suite 1275
Washington D.C. 20036
410-822-0697
www.dfmc.org

Florida

Florida Medical Quality Assurance, Inc.
4350 West Cypress Street, Suite 900
Tampa, Florida 33607
813-354-9111
www.fmqai.com

Georgia

Georgia Medical Care Foundation
57 Executive Park South, Suite 200
Atlanta, Georgia 30329
404-982-0411
www.gmcf.org

Hawaii
American Samoa
Guam

Mountain-Pacific Quality Health Foundation
400 North Park, 2nd Floor
Helena, Montana 59601
406-443-4020
www.mt.net/~mtwy

Idaho

PRO-West/Idaho
720 Park Blvd., Suite 120
Boise, Idaho 83712
208-343-4617
www.pro-west.org

Illinois

Illinois Foundation for Medical Care (Medicare)
2625 Butterfield Road, Suite 104S
Oakbrook, IL 60523
630-571-5540
www.ifmc.org

CIMRO (Medicaid)
100 Trade Centre Drive, Suite 401
Champaign, IL 61820
217-352-1060
www.cimro.com

Indiana

Health Care Excel, Inc.
2901 Ohio Blvd., Suite 112
Terre Haute, IN 47803
812-234-1499
www.hce.org

Iowa

Iowa Foundation for Medical Care
6000 Westown Parkway, Suite 350E
West Des Moines, Iowa 50266
515-223-2900
www.ifmc.org

Kansas

Kansas Foundation for Medical Care, Inc.
2947 S.W. Wanamaker Drive
Topeka, Kansas 66614
785-273-2552
www.kfmc.org

Kentucky

Health Care Excel
P.O. Box 23540
Louisville, Kentucky 40222
502-339-7442
www.hce.org

Louisiana

Louisiana Health Care Review, Inc.
8591 United Plaza Blvd., Suite 270
Baton Rouge, Louisiana 70809
225-926-6353
www.lhcr.org

Maine	Northeast Health Care Quality Foundation 15 Old Rollinsford Road, Suite 302 Dover, New Hampshire 03820 603-749-1641 www.medicarequality.org
Maryland	Delmarva Foundation for Medical Care, Inc. 9240 Centreville Road Easton, Maryland 21601 410-822-0697 www.dfmc.org
Massachusetts	MassPRO 235 Wyman Street Waltham, Massachusetts 02451 617-890-0011 www.masspro.org
Michigan	Michigan Peer Review Organization 40600 An Arbor Road, Suite 200 Plymouth, Michigan 48170 734-459-0900 www.mpro.org
Minnesota	Stratis Health 2901 Metro Drive, Suite 400 Bloomington, Minnesota 55425 612-854-3306 www.stratishealth.org
Mississippi	Information and Quality Healthcare 385 Highland Colony Parkway, Suite 120 Ridgeland, Mississippi 39157 601-957-1575 www.iqh.org

Missouri   Missouri Patient Care Review Foundation (Medicare)
                                505 Hobbs Road, Suite 100
                                Jefferson City, Missouri 65109
                                573-893-7900
                                www.mpcrf.org/MU

                                CIMRO (Medicaid)
                                100 Trade Centre Drive, Suite 401
                                Champaign, IL 61820
                                217-352-1060
                                www.cimro.com

Montana   Mountain-Pacific Quality Health Foundation
                                400 North Park, 2nd Floor
                                Helena, Montana 59601
                                406-443-4020
                                www.mt.net/~mtwy

Nebraska   Iowa Foundation for Medical Care
                                6000 Westown Parkway, Suite 350E
                                West Des Moines, Iowa 50266
                                515-223-2900
                                www.ifmc.org

Nevada   HealthInsight
                                4600 Kietzke Lane, Suite O-269
                                Reno, Nevada 89502
                                702-826-1996
                                www.healthinsight.org

New Hampshire   Northeast Health Care Quality Foundation
                                15 Old Rollinsford Road, Suite 302
                                Dover, New Hampshire 03820
                                603-749-1641
                                www.medicarequality.org

New Jersey	Peer Review Organization of New Jersey 557 Cranbury Road, Suite 21 East Brunswick, New Jersey 08816 732-238-5570 www.pronj.org
New Mexico	New Mexico Medical Review Association P.O. Box 3200 Albuquerque, New Mexico 87190 505-998-9898 www.nmmra.org
New York	Island Peer Review Organization 1979 Marcus Avenue, 1st Floor Lake Success, New York 11042 516-326-7767 www.ipro.org
North Carolina	Medical Review of North Carolina, Inc. 5625 Dilliard Drive, Suite 203 Cary, North Carolina 27511 919-851-2955 www.mrnc.org
North Dakota	North Dakota Health Care Review, Inc. 800 31st Avenue, SW Minot, North Dakota 58701 701-852-4231 www.ndhcri.org
Ohio	Peer Review Systems 757 Brooksedge Plaza Drive Westerville, Ohio 43081 614-895-9900 www.keproinc.com

Oklahoma   Oklahoma Foundation for Medical Quality
                                 5801 Broadway Extension
                                 The Paragon Building, Suite 400
                                 Oklahoma City, Oklahoma 73118
                                 405-840-2891
                                 www.ofmq.com

Oregon   Oregon Medical Professional Review Organization
                                 1220 S.W. 4th, Suite 520
                                 Portland, Oregon 97201
                                 503-279-0100
                                 www.ompro.org

Pennsylvania   KePRO
                                 P.O. Box 8310
                                 Harrisburg, Pennsylvania 17105
                                 717-564-8288
                                 www.keproinc.com

Puerto Rico   Quality Improvement Professional Research Organizatic
                                 Mercantile Plaza, Suite 605
                                 Hato Rey, Puerto Rico 00918
                                 787-641-1240
                                 http://netdial.caribe.net/~qipro

Rhode Island   Rhode Island Quality Partners, Inc.
                                 9 Hayes Street
                                 Providence, Rhode Island 02908
                                 401-528-3200

South Carolina   Carolina Medical Review
                                 A division of Medical Review Of North Carolina
                                 205 Berryhill Road, Suite 101
                                 Columbia, South Carolina 29210
                                 803-731-8225
                                 www.mrnc.org

South Dakota

South Dakota Foundation for Medical Care
1323 S. Minnesota Avenue
Sioux Falls, South Dakota 57105
605-336-3505
www.sdfmc.org

Tennessee

Mid South Foundation for Medical Care, Inc.
6401 Poplar Avenue, Suite 400
Memphis, Tennessee 38119
901-682-0381
www.tnproqio.com

Texas

Texas Medical Foundation
901 Mopac Expressway South
Barton Oaks Plaza Two, Suite 200
Austin, Texas 78746
512-329-6610
www.tmf.org

Utah

HealthInsight
675 E. 2100 South, Suite 270
Salt Lake City, Utah 84106
801-487-2290
www.healthinsight.org

Vermont

Northeast Health Care Quality Foundation
15 Old Rollinsford Road, Suite 302
Dover, New Hampshire 03820
603-749-1641
www.medicarequality.org

Virgin Islands

Virgin Islands Medical Institute
5989 Sunny Isle
St. Croix, Virgin Islands 00823
809-778-6470
www.networkvi.com/vimi/

Virginia   Virginia Health Quality Center
                                1604 Santa Rosa Road, Suite 200
                                Richmond, Virginia 23229
                                804-289-5320
                                www.vhqc.org

Washington   PRO-West
                                10700 Meridian Avenue North, Suite 100
                                Seattle, Washington 98133
                                206-364-9700
                                www.pro-west.org

West Virginia   West Virginia Medical Institute
                                3001 Chesterfield Place
                                Charleston, West Virginia 25304
                                304-346-9864
                                www.wvmi.org

Wisconsin   MetaStar
                                2909 Landmark Place
                                Madison, Wisconsin 53713
                                608-274-1940
                                www.metastar.com

Wyoming   Mountain-Pacific Quality Health Foundation
                                400 North Park, 2nd Floor
                                Helena, Montana 59601
                                307-778-8404
                                www.mt.net/~mtwy

Afterword

$$\blacktriangledown$$

The goal of this book is to provide an introduction of the peer review system to all people working with the organizations, whether they are aware of doing so or not. Unfortunately, it would be impossible to write a detailed study of every review organization and the complex processes they have.

This book is a starting point, not a comprehensive explanation of all the information to be gained about the Peer Review Organizations. Each organization is unique and is the best resource to turn to when a billing or citation question is raised.

Every provider of medical services should be informed of the expectations they work under. Informing staff nurses of criteria and how to document for an external review will not encourage fraudulent charting; it will foster teamwork and effective written communication skills. The staff nurses are merely in need of education of the system and how to document with an external audience in mind, not what to chart to get an approval.

For those already familiar with the Peer Review Organization, it is the goal of this book to make the job of interacting with the organizations easier and more profitable for your institution. Denials of payment and quality of care citations as a result of poor documentation happen every day.

Utilization and quality assurance nurses can be a resource for their facilities to decrease the number of cases referred for physician review, not just deal with denials.

With increased knowledge of the peer review process and coming together to share ideas for improvement, there is a greater chance of the system working more effectively for all participants. The peer review process is not a perfect system.

When the decisions are based on individual medical opinion and not one set of rules that everyone must follow, there will be some cases treated more fairly than others. That is always going to be a part of the process. Although the system lacks in consistency, the peer review process does draws on the expertise and judgment of thousands of physicians and medical professionals in the United States.

A single set of criteria to be used by both Medicare and Medicaid would go a long ways to improving the system and reducing contradictory requirements that result in needless denials of payment and quality of care citations to physicians trying to navigate between the contradictions. A single set of criteria would also help the hospitals by reducing training time for multiple sets of criteria or the endless number of forms that need to be filled out by both government programs to show compliance.

Input from physicians and facilities subject to review could help streamline procedures and decrease the long waiting period for reimbursement. Collaboration could also decrease the number of quality citations that are a result of variations in practice settings or documentation standards, not medical error.

Learning the expectation and policies of the Peer Review Organization will make it easier to prevent review errors from resulting in payment denials or quality citations and expensive corrective action plans. Due diligence is the responsibility of all parties involved in the review process.

Consistent peer review may not be possible, but fair and impartial reviews should be the goal of the reviewer, the review organization and the professionals being reviewed. That requires cooperation on both sides and a willingness to work with the system for improvement.

ABOUT THE AUTHOR

▼

Lisa Raymond, RN, BA, LNC is a legal nurse consultant with a private practice in Sidney, IL. Her previous position was as the Medical Review Analyst at CIMRO, the Illinois Medicaid Peer Review Organization where she conducted utilization reviews, quality of care reviews, and was a member of the diabetes focused-quality study team.

She lives with her husband, Tim and their three sons in Sidney.

NOTES

NOTES

NOTES

NOTES

NOTES

NOTES

NOTES

NOTES

NOTES

▼